Beyond the New World Order

Rick Thomas

rick7homas@protonmail.com
www.victorycanada.today

Beyond the New World Order

© 2022 Rick Thomas. All rights reserved.

No part of this publication may be reproduced, stored in a retrieval system, or transmitted in any form or by any means, electronic, mechanical, photocopying, recording, scanning, or otherwise, without the prior written permission of the author.

We teachers can only help the work going on, as servants wait upon a master. *We then become witnesses to the development of the human soul; the emergence of the New Man who will no longer be the victim of events but, thanks to his clarity of vision, will become able to direct and to mold the future of mankind.*

~ Maria Montessori

I can zero in on a vision of where I want to be in the future. *I can see it so clearly in front of me, when I daydream, it's almost a reality. Then I get this easy feeling, and I don't have to be uptight to get there because I already feel like I'm there, that it's just a matter of time.*

~ Arnold Schwarzenegger

We can no longer stand at the end of something we visualized in detail and plan backwards from that future. *Instead we must stand at the beginning, clear in our mind, with a willingness to be involved in discovery... it asks that we participate rather than plan.*

~ Margaret J. Wheatley

For I dipped into the future, *far as human eye could see, Saw the Vision of the world, and all the wonder that would be.*

~ Alfred Lord Tennyson

Vision is perhaps our greatest strength... *it has kept us alive to the power and continuity of thought through the centuries, it makes us peer into the future and lends shape to the unknown.*

~ Li Ka-shing

When evil men plot, good men must plan. *When evil men burn and bomb, good men must build and bind. When* *evil men shout ugly words of hatred, good men must commit themselves to the glories of love.*

~ Martin Luther King, Jr.

Dear friends, something is happening. *The entrenched front of the makers of corona is crumbling and dissolving. And that is because the power of US. The power of humanity is greater than the power of those on the other side, the inhumans. Humanity with emotions will always prevail over digitalization and artificial intelligence. We are obviously dealing here with megalomaniac psychopaths and sociopaths who should have been stopped a long time ago. But now the time has come for this. That is why millions of people are demonstrating all over the world today. That's what this is all about. It is humanity versus inhumanity. We are human. We can laugh, cry, sing, dance and hug. The other side can't. Because the other side has no access to the spiritual side.* **Therefore, without any doubt, the other — dark side — will lose this inhuman battle against life and creation.**

~ Dr. Reiner Fuellmich

Contents

1 / A Vision of the Future
2 / Natural Health
3 / Manufacturing the State
4 / Dinosaurs
5 / A New Constitution
6 / Breaking Down Barriers
7 / Cats & Dogs
8 / A World United
9 / The Resistance
10 / The New Spiritualists
Epilogue / Empowered Communities

ONE / A Vision of the Future

The plandemic of 2020 and the draconian response of virtually all national governments has revealed, in glaring detail, the flaws, faults, divisions and entrenched corruption not only in the West, but also in governments all around the world. If there was ever any doubt that our sociopathic overlords are criminally insane, these doubts have been swept aside. If we combined Stalin, Hitler and Mao into one human being and then cloned another 10,000 of them, we would have a close approximation of our enemies.

And yet, our faith in the immutable and eternal benevolence of our Creator, compels us to press forward in outrageous confidence; we shall overcome and we shall triumph in a manner far beyond the brilliant expectations of our most cherished dreamers. Nothing can withstand the will of the people.

Yet, how do we even begin to have a discussion of life-after-pandemic when we are assaulted on all sides, hemmed in and under attack? It is like sitting in the trenches of World War One, trying to write a utopian novel of the future while bombs are dropping on all sides—and this scenario is made all the more bittersweet because utopian novels are invariably pipe dreams wreathed in fantasy and wishful thinking.

Therefore, our vision of the future must be practical and doable; complete with a clearcut plan that anyone can follow. This book is an attempt to do just that. It's a plan we can begin now, no need to wait for the Empire of Chaos to crumble and fall. In fact, planting the seeds of the new world will help destroy their misguided agenda and take us Beyond the New World Order.

Fascination of the Abomination

"Hell is empty and all the devils are here."

~ *William Shakespeare*

Some things need to be cleared up before we can launch into any discussion of our vision of the future. The Freedom Movement is currently being inundated with an overwhelming deluge of information from a growing multitude of sources: doctors, independent journalists, historians, nurses, Facebook posts, chat groups, podcasts, lawyers and countless concerned citizens stepping forward to present evidence of the global crimes against humanity brought on by the plandemic, the dangerous mRNA injections and the lockdown of economies all over the world.

Social media is bombarded with new and more horrifying information everyday about the vaccine injuries and deaths, and the nefarious ingredients of the mRNA injections. Combined with this, are the daily reports of further restrictions, quarantine camps and police brutality against Freedom Movement protestors all over the world.

There is a human tendency to become fascinated with evil; it is the same morbid fascination people have driving past a car wreck or watching horror movies. Joseph Conrad referred to it as the *"fascination of the abomination"* in his novel *The Heart of Darkness*. Dr. Jeffrey Goldstein, a professor of social and organizational psychology at the University of Utrecht was quoted in a 2013 interview as saying:

"People go to horror films because they want to be frightened or they wouldn't do it twice. You choose your entertainment because you want it to affect you. That's certainly true of people who go to entertainment products like horror films that have big effects. They want those effects...[Horror films must] provide a just resolution in the end. The bad guy gets it. Even though they choose to watch these things, the images are still disturbing for many people. But people have the ability to pay attention as much or as little as they care to in order to control what effect it has on them, emotionally and otherwise."

The psychoanalyst Dr. Carl Jung believed horror films *"...tapped into primordial archetypes buried deep in our collective subconscious – images like shadow and mother play an important role in the horror genre".*

Jung called the inner evil within human beings *the shadow*, which is the unconscious part of our personality that our conscious ego does not identify in itself, or the entirety of the unconscious; that is, everything of which a person is not fully conscious. We could say the shadow is our unknown side.

One of the blind spots of human beings is their inability to see evil in themselves. *All men think in their hearts they are right but God ponders the soul.* Most of the wrong-doing in the world is unconscious and people deflect their own wrong-doing through their morbid fascination with evil behavior in others. Otherwise, known as projection.

What we are watching in real time is a live horror movie that could easily be the subject of any number of apocalyptic films. Part of the paralysis that is gripping many in our movement is this morbid fascination and obsession with evil. Evil is a bottomless pit and we cannot be helpful to the movement if we are continually staring into the abyss. We need solutions and answers, and we also need organization, unity and planning to win this war. We also desperately need a vision of the future.

We all need to realize and understand that there is something dysfunctional about all of our institutions, governments and nations. The system is breaking down, families are breaking down. We have an opioid crisis, homelessness is growing, depression and suicide have escalated over the last two years.

Our institutions, governments and politicians are economically and morally bankrupt. We cannot draw on the bank account of the international system any longer.

However, the good news is that we are not spiritually bankrupt. The Well of the Spirit is deep and we can draw on it any time without fear of depleting it. The Bank of the Spirit can pay out dividends to all of those who invest their spiritual resources in it, and the return on the investment is exponential. A small amount deposited in this bank can grow into a mighty reserve. As the wise carpenter from Nazareth once said,

"The kingdom of heaven is like a grain of mustard seed which a man sowed in his field. Now a mustard seed is the least of seeds, but when it is full grown, it becomes the greatest of all herbs and is like a tree so that the birds of heaven are able to come and rest in the branches thereof."

United We Stand

"Unity is strength... when there is teamwork and collaboration, wonderful things can be achieved."

~ Mattie Stepanek

One of the most wonderful things that has occurred because of the plandemic of 2020 and the resulting government restrictions, is that all the like-minded people were drawn together. The vast majority of us had never met each other before this all happened and most likely would never have met. We would have remained in our little isolated worlds, doing our thing and living our lives.

We come from a variety of backgrounds, occupations, faiths and interests. We have in common an awareness of the inherent evil that exists behind the government, media, pharmaceutical companies, banks and corporations. We also understand the agenda that is powering the plandemic and the Elites' insane goals for world domination.

Now that we are together, now that we've found each other, what are we supposed to do together? The most obvious answer is that we are supposed to work together to defeat the vaccine passports, health mandates and restore our civil rights. We must unite on a global scale to defeat our global enemies, and this is an enormous challenge, but it is not all that needs to be done. We must also bring the perpetrators to trial and this, too, is not an easy task. The tentacles of the western establishment are far-reaching and all-pervading and the Empire controls the justice system, the economic system, the political system and just about everything else including the media, education, police and military.

The good news is that the harder they push to achieve their goals, the greater the resistance will be, and the more they squeeze our community together the more united and strong we will become. So when they bully, coerce and manipulate us, we say "Bring it on!"

Unity does not come from all of us thinking the same, believing the same and acting the same: that's uniformity, not unity. We are not robots nor should we be aiming for robotic, dogmatic behavior from our community. We are united by our common goals, by our common spiritual destiny and the common inner spirit that compels us all to stand up and speak out against tyranny. Focus on these things and everything else will be much easier.

The dictionary definition of unity:

1. The state or quality of being one or united into a whole.
2. The state or quality of being in accord; harmony.

The key to this is the word *harmony*. In music the combination of different musical notes played or sung at the same time to produce a pleasing sound is called harmony. People working together in different ways and projects creates harmony of purpose. Deity is known by its harmony and unity; the universe always works together as one. Even the most cursory look at the stars in heaven reveals an orderly creation of whirling planets revolving around mother suns, organized in galaxies.

Rick Thomas

When the entire Freedom Movement becomes interconnected around the whole world, working together in harmony with unity of purpose, we will be an unstoppable force, an army of unprecedented size, power and will. It is the challenge of our entire global movement to break down all barriers that stand in the way of the ultimate goal of winning this war.

TWO / Natural Health

The Freedom Movement is virtually unanimous in the shared belief that every individual is responsible for their own health; we are also unanimous that the government has no rights, claims or authority over our bodies; nor can governments force its citizens to take medical treatments. We all agree these vaccine mandates are illegal, unconstitutional and immoral, and furthermore, the science and available data is showing that these mRNA injections are dangerous.

The western medical establishment and its philosophy of medicine are the end products of the Enlightenment thinkers who rejected conventional natural medicine in favor of a more empirical model based on science and the scientific method. This philosophy of medicine is rooted in materialism.

Materialism says that the physical world is all there is, and therefore an individual is a biological machine, created by nature. Materialism rejects the spiritual world because it is outside the realm of empirical science and therefore, according to materialists, the concept of a soul, eternal life or a spiritual world is not valid. "Science" has become the arbitrator and judge of all truth.

Materialistic modern medicine views natural or holistic medicine as unscientific but our philosophy of medicine is rooted in the natural or holistic health tradition that views the whole person, his or her body, mind and soul. A human being is not an isolated biological anomaly—we are all interconnected through the spirit, part of a universal community. We are not just biological automatons or accidental freaks of nature. Life is purposeful and meaningful, and our mind, body and soul are connected, not only inwardly, but also we are also connected to the universe and to each other.

Alchemy Therapies — Natural medicine vs conventional Western

Natural	Conventional
Works with body to by strengthening natural defences. Focus on **health**	Target-driven approach on pathogen – e.g. 'magic bullet'. Focus on **disease**
Deals with **causes** – treat underlying root causes of disease using natural interventions on mind, body and spirit	Deals with **symptoms** – suppression or 'management' via predominantly pharmaceutical and surgical means
Empowers person to heal themselves; Treats **person** not the disease	Gives power to medical 'experts'. Treats **disease** regardless of person
Requires commitment and **taking responsibility** for oneself	Allows person to **avoid responsibility** and 'keep taking the tablets'
Good for **chronic** illness where disease is ideopathic and multifactorial	Good for **acute** illness e.g infectious disease with clear single target

Materialistic medicine treats symptoms with pharmaceutical remedies—pharmacology is really a war against the body whereas natural medicine is interested in creating peace and harmony in an individual's emotional, mental, physical and spiritual self. The goal of pharmaceutical medicine is to stop symptoms from manifesting. The goal of holistic medicine is to improve the overall health and happiness of the person.

Materialistic medicine views the unhealthy as social aberrations in the context of the state because universal healthcare practiced by western democracies is entrenched in the pharmaceutical model of medicine. The health of the citizens is therefore the responsibility of the state.

Holistic medicine puts the responsibility for health on the individual, not the state. The state is therefore threatened by holistic medicine because it undermines the monopoly of health that the state claims it has rightful authority over. The current pandemic has brought into sharp focus these conflicting philosophies.

Our holistic model of health and medicine is more humane and will eventually triumph over pharmaceutical medicine. This needs to be said. Our Freedom Movement may be the catalyst to overthrow the dominance of the pharmaceutical industry's monopoly. Things are already changing in people's attitude toward Big Pharma.

In a recent interview with Healthline, Dr. Andrew Weil, creator of the Program in Integrative Medicine at the University of Arizona is on record as saying:

"Patients are dissatisfied with the small amount of time they get with their doctors and with doctors who prescribe a pill for every ill," Weil said. "The integrative medicine movement is not a rejection of conventional methods. But patients are saying that the conventional model is not working, that it's broken. And they are right."

https://www.healthline.com/health-news/alternative-medicine-becoming-mainstream#Proponents:-The-Time-Has-Come

The best defense against disease is a healthy lifestyle of proper diet and nutrition, sleep and exercise. This simple truth is gaining more and more acceptance all over the world as countries with populations that embrace a healthy lifestyle consistently, year after year, report higher life expectancy and happier people.

S.NO.	HOMEOPATHY	ALLOPATHY
1.	Homeopathy is based on the concept that 'the source which has caused the ailment will cure it.'	Allopathy is based on a belief/ concept, i.e., 'the cure is other than the cause.'
2.	Homeopathic medicines take a little bit of time to relieve the patient from the ailment. Homeopathic medicines do not give instant results.	On the other hand, allopathy relieves the patient instantly, but it comes with its own share of side-effects.
3.	Homeopathy believes in the concept of curing the body and bringing out a change in it so that it can function in a better way.	Allopathy believes in giving instant relief to the patient through the use of drugs.
4.	Homeopathy does not harm the body in any way. It focuses on treating the past ailments along with the new ones.	On the other hand, allopathy is concerned with treating a particular body part that has been hampered due to the ailment. But in treating the disease, it has its share of side-effects.
5.	Homeopathic doctors believe that an imbalance in mental and emotional causes several ailments in patients. The doctors in homeopathy treat the diseases with the smallest dose of medicines which does not affect the immune system.	Allopathy is known as a 'double edge sword' because the doctors are heavily dependent upon the drugs for treating the disease.
6.	Homeopathy has always been a pain-free treatment wherein the patients are given small doses of medicines.	Allopathy includes painful treatments wherein several machines are attached to the patient.

A simple study of countries with the highest life expectancy reveals Japan consistently at the top of the list (average life expectancy is 84 years old) because, simply put, the Japanese eat very well—they eat fish versus red meat, eat less dairy, butter, and milk, eat seaweed that is high in iodine, drink a lot of green tea, eat plenty of vegetables, and consume small portions.

Does that mean that universal healthcare is the problem? Not necessarily, because we could just as easily have a universal healthcare system based on holistic medicine where people paid into a system designed to prevent them from becoming ill instead of a system designed to profit from sickness.

Deceptology

According to health writer Jon Barron:

"In terms of surgical technique (the cutting apart and repair of the human body) modern medicine has made remarkable advances. In terms of identifying many of the germs that play a role in causing many diseases and improving sanitation to prevent those diseases, once again modern medicine has made remarkable advances. In terms of burns, trauma, and ER's, modern medicine is nothing short of miraculous. But in terms of treating and preventing most disease, particularly the major scourges of the modern era (heart disease, cancer, diabetes, osteoporosis, and Alzheimer's) modern medicine stands an abject failure."

https://www.jonbarron.org/article/why-your-doctors-do-you-they-do

The horrible truth emerging from the investigations of many medical scientists and health professionals is that an epidemic of corruption in the pharmaceutical industry has resulted in an increase in a variety of diseases that were either infrequent or unknown a hundred years ago.

In a peer-reviewed article submitted to the National Center of Biotechnology Information in December of 2020 (and since retracted for obvious reasons by the NCBI) the author states that, *"Four generations of drug-dependent Americans strongly suggest that medical establishment has practiced decades of intellectual deception."* Furthermore, the vaccine rollout of the last few decades has exacerbated and created more disease but maybe that was the plan all along.

Plant Medicine	vs Drugs
Shared by	*Marc Schrueder*
Natural, from nature	Synthetic, unnatural
Amplify, support, moderate	Block, suppress, obstruct
Detoxify	Toxify
Multidimensional	One-dimensional
Homeostatic intelligence	Programmed robots
Sensitize receptor sites	Confuse, clog receptor sites
Supports immunity	Depress immunity
Reduce inflammation	Cause inflammation
Attack only harmful bacteria	Attack indiscriminately

Young Living Event, Philippines

This statement has not been evaluated by the Food and Drug Administration. This product is not intended to diagnose, treat, cure or prevent disease.

"From Rockefeller's support of patent medicine to Gates' patent vaccines, medical establishment invested a great deal in intellectual ignorance. Through the control over medical education and research it has created a public illusion to prop up corporate profit and encouraged the lust for money and power. An overview of data on cancer and vaccine sciences, the status of Americans' health, a survey of repeated failed projects, economic toxicity, and heavy drug consumption or addiction among young and old provide compelling evidence that in the twentieth century nearly all classic disease categories (congenital, inheritance, neonatal, or induced) shifted to increase induced diseases."

https://www.ncbi.nlm.nih.gov/pmc/articles/PMC7749544/

There is no contest to the argument that our Freedom Movement's Healthcare philosophy is superior to the corrupt pharmaceutical industry's Death-care system. All that needs to be done is informing the public of the corruption in the system and at the same time sharing our proposal to replace pharmaceutical medicine with the much more humane and compassionate holistic model.

That does not mean we have to throw out everything that our current modern medical system has to offer. Keep the things that are actually working, such as advanced surgery techniques, burns and trauma medicine; and combine the sophisticated tech, like MRI machines, with the holistic approach. Good medicine is still good medicine. If it is effective in helping to alleviate human suffering, then it matters not what model or method is applied.

THREE / Manufacturing the State

History shows that all civilizations have similar evolutions on the road from tribal society to the modern nation-state. First comes the family, followed by the clan, the tribe, the farming village, the trading town, the city center, the city-state, the feudal monarchy and finally arriving at the modern nation-states that we witness around the world today. If we wanted to manufacture a state from scratch we would go through the same steps beginning with the family unit.

Family

The family is both the fundamental unit of society as well as the root of culture. It is a perpetual source of encouragement, advocacy, assurance, and emotional refueling that empowers a child to venture with confidence into the greater world and to become all that he can be.

~ Marianne E. Neifert, Dr. Mom's Parenting Guide

A family in harmony will prosper in everything.

~ Chinese Proverb

The basic building block of society is the family—it being the smallest social group held together by mutual bonds of interdependence: the helpless child dependent primarily on its mother; the mother dependent on the father, especially during the child-bearing and early years of infancy. The father is bonded to the family by his need for community, belonging and more practically, by sex-craving and the security and comfort that a home can provide.

From humankind's earliest days, the family has been the cornerstone of society. Families grew into extended families and clans became tribes. When the nomadic hunter-gatherers settled down to become an agricultural community, they developed taboos, customs and a rough legal code that all members were obligated to follow.

Agriculture provided permanence, something that nomadic hunter-gatherers did not experience. This permanence allowed for the evolution of society: simple government by a council of elders, marital customs, religious laws, and the development of basic rules governing property and the exchange of goods developed.

Villages became towns and then cities, and those city-states grew into nations and nation-states until over the course of thousands of years we evolved into the complex, diverse, technologically advanced, socially challenged and increasingly integrated global civilization.

In the West, the family has borne the brunt of the deteriorating slide of our civilization. Without healthy, functioning families, Western society is doomed to decline and deteriorate.

Healthy, functioning families produce healthy, functioning children who enter life prepared and poised to contribute significantly to the social, cultural, economic, political and religious well-being of the nation. And conversely, unhealthy, dysfunctional families produce unhealthy, dysfunctional children who often create havoc, sorrow and more dysfunction.

The breakdown of the family prevents civilization from advancing—divorce is the brake that slows down the forward progress of a nation or society.

Tabula Rasa

An insect is born with everything it needs to know; it does not require any training or education by its parents, but human beings are born *tabula rasa*, which is Greek for *blank slate*.

Human beings are not born with the necessary skills or knowledge to survive. Family is the transfer agent for conveying the skills, customs and attitudes that every child needs to survive and thrive in society. The values and ideals of a society must be taught fresh with each new generation. Unless there is adequate parenting within the society, the nation will not progress; unless the previous generation successfully transfers the cultural values and meanings to the next generation, the society will decline. Any interruption or distortion of this transfer will negatively impact the child.

Divorce results in a suspension or retrogression in the advancement of culture for the simple reason that the child is raised by only one parent and does not benefit from the advantage of two parents, one male and one female, transferring their unique and comprehensive view of life. The stability of the home life is also inimical to the further progress of the individual, and the emotional and mental stress of divorce placed upon the child hampers and retards the progress of the child as he or she grows to be an adult.

The family and local community network of friends, teachers and acquaintances provides the foundation for all the cultural knowledge and social values that a growing individual needs to function and thrive in the society. The quality of parenting is directly proportional to the quality of the nation as a whole.

Institutional parenting centers are wholly inadequate to enable the development of children. Any and all attempts to circumvent or substitute the family with state-controlled centers of child-rearing will only result in disaster for the society as a whole. There is no substitute for mom and dad.

Brotherhood

The family is the ideal vehicle to promote those values and meanings which aid and enhance the underlying social glue which we call *brotherhood*. If we want a unified, peaceful world, then the family is the best starting place to foster higher human values of tolerance, kindness, generosity, peacefulness and co-operation.

Children who are taught that all men and women are our brothers and sisters and that, just as they are part of a small local family, so, too they are part of a world-wide extended family, are far better prepared for a productive, healthy life in the community than those who are taught the pursuit of self-gratification and the stock-piling of material possessions.

Religion plays an essential role in the fostering of universal ideals of the common good and well-being of all. Religion taught in the home provides the child with the far-reaching and far-seeing view of eternity—that he or she is also part of a much greater, boundless, endless existence and that their initial life is only the starting point of a much greater adventure that awaits them. Such values of human brotherhood are essential for the establishing of an international sense of affection for all mankind.

Marriage

"There is nothing more lovely in life than the union of two people whose love for one another has grown through the years, from the small acorn of passion, into a great rooted tree."

~ *Vita Sackville-West*

Marriage is the core building block of values because marriage teaches young men and women to put the interests of others ahead of their own through parenting. The consistent love and devotion necessary to ensure successful parenting creates a better person. Marriage requires adapting and adjusting to another's social behavior; it teaches patience, kindness and empathy for the struggles of other less mature beings.

Marriage requires the giving-up of reckless pursuits, the stifling of unbridled passion, and the forgetting of self. Selfish, spoiled young people do not make for good parenting, nor are they adequately prepared to raise children.

Family is the great testing ground for future life. It teaches compromise and tolerance: children, as well as parents, learn to interact peacefully within the group.

The state can never be adequate surrogate parents nor can it hope to provide the necessary environment to foster the growth and maturity of youth. The state's job ought to be to foster, encourage and protect the family but not rule over it.

Agriculture

"The first farmer was the first man. All historic nobility rests on the possession and use of land."

~ *Ralph Waldo Emerson*

"Whenever there are in any country uncultivated lands and unemployed poor, it is clear that the laws of property have been so far extended as to violate natural right. The earth is given as a common stock for man to labour and live on. The small landowners are the most precious part of a state."

~ *Thomas Jefferson*

Civilization began when hunter-gathers gave up their nomadic existence and planted crops about 12,000 years ago. The earliest agriculture was most likely a small forest garden tended by the family members. Reliance on the soil to supplement a diet of meat, nuts and berries was a big leap forward for primitive man.

Farming provided a food surplus that enabled primitive humans time to pursue and develop other activities such as pottery, blacksmithing and looming. Farming also required less manpower than hunting and gathering and this freed up labour for other tasks that greatly enhanced the survival factor of small tribes and families.

Agriculture provided permanence, something the nomadic hunter-gatherer tribes did not experience. This permanence allowed for the evolution of society: simple government by a council of elders; marital customs; religious customs and basic rules governing property and the exchange of goods developed. Permanence allowed man to build on his previous ideas, to evolve.

Permanence greatly aided the development of the family unit by providing much needed stability and social cohesiveness. The child gained the added advantage of increased security and social integration.

In a nutshell, agriculture provided for the following improvements in human life:
- Improved irrigation and food storage technologies that provided food surplus
- Domestication of animals
- Use of animal fertilizer
- Higher population density
- Labour diversification
- Trading economies
- Development of art, architecture and culture
- Centralized administration and political structures
- Development of religious and political ideology
- Property laws
- Writing

The Family Farm

Looking forward, in modern times, the family farm is a great stabilizer of community. The advent of large-scale commercial farming has greatly reduced the number of family farms, not only in the west but also in Asia. The decline of the family farm is a serious indicator of the breakdown and devolution of society.

Family farmers are more responsible care-takers of the land: they live and work on the land and are more concerned for the long-term effects on the soil and water systems. They have a vested interest in preserving the land for future generations. Family farmers use far less pesticides and harmful chemical fertilizers.

Local farms produce healthier food leading to a community of healthier people with fewer incidences of illness and disease.

Local farmers buy and hire workers locally that benefits the local economy. Large-scale corporate farming pollutes the land with pesticides and exhaust from heavy machinery. Factory farming of animals uses antibiotics, hormones and bleach to kill bacteria and enhance growth.

The use of GMO seeds has greatly increased the level of cancer worldwide, some studies showing a doubling of cancer rates. The consumption of hormone-treated beef can cause girls to prematurely enter puberty, which makes them more susceptible to breast and other cancers.

Large-scale industrial operations require the use of lagoons or storage pits for the excessive amounts of manure produced by congregating livestock in small areas. The manure harms the environment by giving off hazardous gases such as ammonia, hydrogen sulphide, and methane.

Local farmers are active in their communities and help promote democratic values and provide society with much needed stability. The reduction of food, crops and livestock to commodity also reduces and dehumanizes the soul-enriching benefits of agriculture.

Agriculture is the most human of activities because it returns and restores us to the soil from whence we came. We are creatures of nature whether we care to admit it or not. Gardening, farming and animal husbandry produces a peace-loving, gentler human being than the predatory hunter that man evolved from.

Private Property

The family farm naturally resulted in the ownership and inheritance of property. Passing down the family farm from one generation to the next greatly enhanced the stability of small emerging towns and villages. Property allowed sons and grandsons an economic future and a historical continuity within the community: a sense of belonging, as well as a shared past and future.

All government, legal systems, rights, civil codes, social privileges, customs, and institutions of peace and happiness that we now know evolved from the private ownership of property—private property made it necessary to establish government to legislate between the various holders of property within the community. This has remained unchanged for thousands of years.

The first small communities of herders set up boundary stones in their fields to mark their property. One of the earliest crimes was moving a neighbor's boundary stones to expand one's own territory. Another was the theft of livestock: it quickly became customary to mark one's livestock to tell it apart from a neighbors in the event of a dispute.

Inheritance laws were formed to regulate who got what after the death of the father or often, property was passed on through the mother. Many societies passed on the inheritance to the oldest son, some to the youngest. Islamic law proscribes that the son to inherit twice as much as the daughter; despite what appears to be unfair and discriminatory to the modern world, this was an improvement at the time, because before that, the daughters got nothing.

As a city-state evolves it develops a transportation system, writing, currency, legal systems, art, architecture, science, metallurgy and religion. All of these developments require division of labor and specialized training for the primary reason that it takes far too long to learn a skill such as pottery or architecture and few individuals have the ability, time or dedication to pursue more than one or two professions in a lifetime.

Human beings crave to own and live on land that they can say belongs to them. Man has an inner need and a psychological desire to find security and a sense of belonging. Due to the brevity of mortal existence, the sense of permanence offers an enhanced sense of well-being to the land-owner—*though the storms may come, the rains may assail me, I will stand firm and protect my inheritance for future generations.*

All trade between neighbors, laws governing the buying and selling of animals and crops, social customs within small agricultural communities stemmed from the ownership of land. The human family, as it evolved under the father-mother bond, rooted itself in the land and formed civil society and government that originated from man on the land.

Disintegration

Civilization in its most basic form is therefore based on *family, agriculture and private property*. The family farm therefore provides all three in one unit. If any one of these three basic building blocks of civilization is either threatened or destroyed, the civilization is in jeopardy.

We have witnessed the disintegration of the family unit in the last one hundred years on an unparalleled scale. Millions have fled the agricultural life in pursuit of greener pastures in urban centers. Private property has likewise been greatly reduced by apartment rental living. Despite the poverty of the feudal serf, he provided great stability to society. The industrial debt-serf does not give similar stability to society and his or her existence is more precarious than the feudal serf.

Whatever institutions, organizations, groups, committees, rallies and ideals or values we preach, they must protect the family, agriculture and private property for the well-being of all citizens. Our current corporate-led world takes little or no consideration of any of these things when decisions are made. Neither do our national governments make laws that are tempered by the question of how they will affect the family.

That needs to change by first of all bringing the family into all discussions, debates and media conversations in the public arena. Secondly, a legislative body needs to be established that governs all issues relating to family, childcare, marriage, divorce and parenting. This body ought to be run by successfully married couples.

Only happy, self-sufficient citizens can change the world. Unhappy citizens, who are dependent on the state, do not make for a strong nation.

Unintended Consequences

Weakening society and nations by the conscious, deliberate scheming of conniving men and women, and with the unconscious acquiescence of the people leads to the unlooked-for harvest of civil unrest, social decay and world wars.

The pursuit of wealth and power with its adjacent abandonment of spiritual values has consequences. War is the inevitable consequence of the breakdown of national relations. Nations fall into disputes over land and resources when they have lost sight of the universal purpose and meaning of life.

If the children of a family were to abandon their parents, and run away from home to start their own society, it would be one of poverty and chaos because children do not have the maturity to rule themselves. The same is true of our global family—abandoning the plans and guidance of our universal Source and Center cannot go well.

FOUR / Dinosaurs

Many of our western institutions need to be reformed or abandoned completely. Monarchy is one of them. Hereditary titles passed on from generation to generation are a throwback to our feudal past. We would never allow our elected leaders to hand down their government positions from generation to generation, yet we allow monarchy to continue because of romantic notions of kings and queens, and knights in shining armor.

The Elites want a hereditary corporate monarchy that will ensure that their progeny will remain in power forever. In order to make this happen, they realize it would be easier to keep a compact population and therefore they have unleashed an engineered virus, just ask Elon Musk:

"An asteroid or a supervolcano could certainly destroy us, but we also face risks the dinosaurs never saw: **An engineered virus***, nuclear war, inadvertent creation of a micro black hole, or some as-yet-unknown technology could spell the end of us."*

We need to create a society where our political leaders, civil servants and bureaucrats are given their positions based on their merits, track record and abilities, not based on their allegiance to their corporate family. The dinosaurs of this age that are facing imminent extinction are threatened by the alternative way of life that those in our Freedom community are proclaiming.

Meritocracy

The party-system of politics also needs to be reconsidered and direct representative democracy established instead, while we work towards the abolishment of political parties. They served us for a time to bridge the gap between our feudal past and modern governments, but they, like the dinosaurs, are facing extinction.

Politicians who represent the people need to actually serve the people and not their political party. Political parties have become political cults, especially witnessed in the United States where there are two cults feuding relentlessly 24/7 on social media—and never the twain shall meet.

Direct autonomous representatives who are elected municipally, provincially and federally need not be constrained or controlled by a party that demands allegiance to a party agenda.

Surveillance State

The death of the surveillance state needs to be proclaimed loud and clear. Collection of data, facial recognition software, street cameras, digital identity and other techno-feudal systems of control need to be outlawed completely. Privacy of our personal information needs to be protected and federal laws created to ban the sharing of data for any purpose.

It needs to be a felony offense to buy and sell personal data, punishable by prison terms and steep fines because data selling is an egregious violation of our civil rights. Amendments of existing charters of rights or new constitutions need to be created that include the right to privacy and protection against data sharing.

"Arguing that you don't care about the right to privacy because you have nothing to hide, is no different than saying you don't care about free speech because you have nothing to say... The common argument that we have 'if you have nothing to hide ...you have nothing to fear'– the origins of that are literally Nazi propaganda... That is literally the origin of that quote. It's from their minister of propaganda Joseph Goebbels. So when we hear modern politicians, when we hear modern people repeating that reflexively without confronting its origins, without confronting what it really says... that's harmful."

~ Edward Snowden

Ponzi Planet

Our western Wall Street/City of London financial system of fractional reserve banking, stock market casino capitalism and the derivatives market all need to go the way of the dinosaurs. Creating wealth out of thin air through organized financial gambling and fractional reserve banking needs to be banned.

The complete overhaul of the global institutions established after WW2 is in order. The World Bank, IMF, World Trade Organization and the Bank of International Settlements (BIS) are private organizations that have no oversight and answer to no one. No person, corporation, nation or society can be permitted to exist or operate outside of international and national law. The central banks need to be restructured.

Our Freedom Movement is very aware of the awful truth that our global economy is a Ponzi-scheme of endless snowballing debt, where old debts are paid off by new debts. Here's an excellent article that goes into more detail:

https://archive.globalpolicy.org/social-and-economic-policy/the-world-economic-crisis/general-analysis-2/51144-ponzi-planet-the-danger-debt-poses-to-the-western-world-.html

The irony of the Elites' 2030 sustainable development goals is that they are *unsustainable* goals and they do not involve development. The debt-based bubble is destined to crash, it is just a matter of time. The Elites are gambling that they can manage an engineered crash and move in their Great Reset digital economy without destroying themselves in the process. The Elites are very aware of the danger they are in—Henry Kissinger warned in an article in the Wall Street Journal at the outset of the pandemic: *"The historic challenge for leaders is to manage the crisis while building the future. Failure could set the world on fire."* The article reads very much like a set of instructions. He opines further, *"The crisis effort, however vast and necessary, must not crowd out the urgent task of launching a parallel enterprise for the transition to the post-coronavirus order."*

https://tzirkotis.wordpress.com/2020/04/05/the-coronavirus-pandemic-will-forever-alter-the-world-order-henry-a-kissinger/

Corporate Media

"When the public's right to know is threatened, and when the rights of free speech and free press are at risk, all of the other liberties we hold dear are endangered."

~ *Christopher Dodd*

In conjunction with the Separation of Corporation and State, the mainstream media needs to be dismantled and de-monopolized along with the social media giants Facebook, Twitter and YouTube. At the very least, Facebook needs to be turned into a non-for-profit public entity managed by public trustees, instead of a tool of censorship, propaganda and control. The other alternative (which is already happening) is to create independent media that takes over the vacuum of true journalism left vacate by the corporate media outlets. CNN's drastic drop in ratings over the last two years is ample proof.

There can be no freedom of speech and freedom of the press if corporate elites control the media and censor dissenting voices. Ideally, a free and independent press is the voice of the people and not the propaganda tool of established tyrants.

All governments whether democratic or totalitarian must use the force of law. Our movement is no different. We must force the implementation of our mandates through all peaceful, lawful means at our disposal. The right to use force—not violence—is part of a just democracy. Our brainwashed fellow citizens cannot be the People because they have no will left, therefore it is up to our Freedom Movement.

Operation Robin Hood

The world's billionaires have seen their wealth surge by over $5.5 trillion since the beginning of the pandemic, a gain of over 68 percent. There are approximately 2700 global billionaires whose combined wealth rose from $8 trillion on March 20, 2020 to $13.5 trillion as of July 31, 2021. We have no idea how much the trillionaires increased their wealth because it is never reported in the media. Forbes' list of the world's billionaires never includes the international bankers and oil company elites such as the Rothschilds and Rockefellers who control trillions in global wealth.

https://www.forbes.com/billionaires/

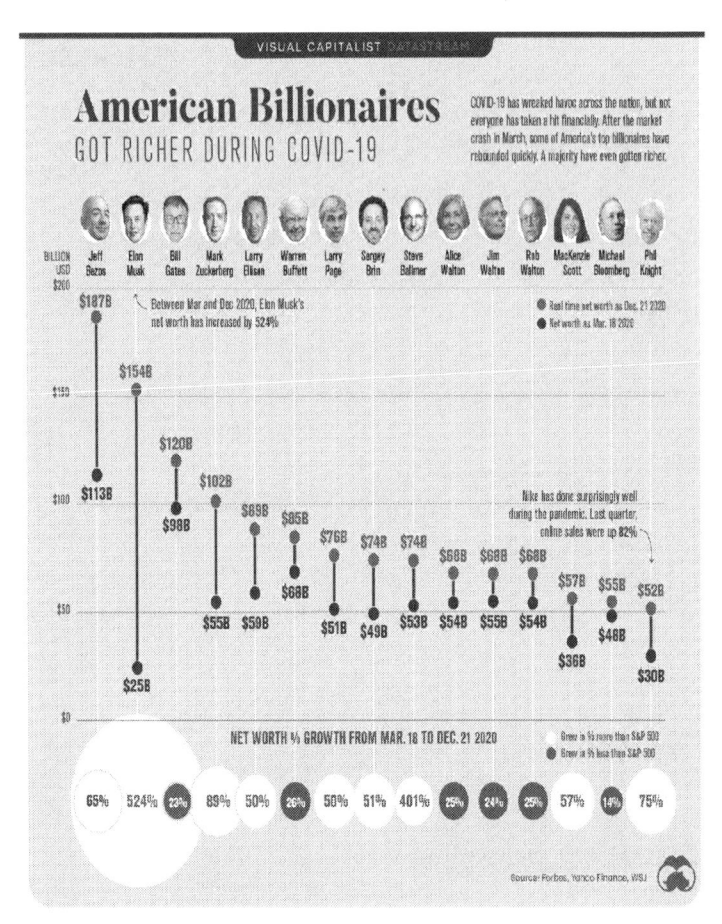

American Billionaires
GOT RICHER DURING COVID-19

COVID-19 has wreaked havoc across the nation, but not everyone has taken a hit financially. After the market crash in March, some of America's top billionaires have rebounded quickly. A majority have even gotten richer.

● Real time net worth as Dec. 21 2020
● Net worth as Mar. 18 2020

Between Mar and Dec 2020, Elon Musk's net worth has increased by 524%

Nike has done surprisingly well during the pandemic. Last quarter, online sales were up 82%

NET WORTH % GROWTH FROM MAR. 18 TO DEC. 21 2020

● Grew in % more than S&P 500
● Grew in % less than S&P 500

Billionaire	Dec 2020	Mar 2020	Growth %
Jeff Bezos	$187B	$113B	65%
Elon Musk	$154B	$25B	524%
Bill Gates	$120B	$98B	23%
Mark Zuckerberg	$102B	$55B	89%
Larry Ellison	$89B	$59B	50%
Warren Buffett	$85B	$68B	26%
Larry Page	$76B	$51B	50%
Sergey Brin	$74B	$49B	51%
Steve Ballmer	$74B	$53B	40%
Alice Walton	$68B	$54B	25%
Jim Walton	$69B	$55B	24%
Rob Walton	$68B	$54B	25%
MacKenzie Scott	$57B	$36B	57%
Michael Bloomberg	$55B	$48B	14%
Phil Knight	$52B	$30B	75%

Source: Forbes, Yahoo Finance, WSJ

Along with the Separation of Corporation and State, which incidentally would undermine both the state control of means of production as well as corporate control of the state, we must also work towards the goal of global re-distribution of wealth and resources. The wealth that has been systematically stolen from the middle and working classes must be returned.

The Global Public Private Partnership

Policy Makers

This is the part of the GPPP where policy originates.

- **B.I.S** — Bank for International Settlements (B.I.S): They ultimately control the money supply and thus global markets, trade and national economies.
- **Central Banks** (Coordinated by the B.I.S): They are "going direct" and directly funding government spending. Monetary policy has effectively become fiscal policy.
- W.E.F., C.F.R, Club of Rome, Chatham House, Rockefellers
- **Think Tanks & Global Representative Groups**: These formulate the policies to achieve GPPP objectives. Resource allocation determined by the B.I.S and Central Banks but they work in in "partnership" with the think tanks and the representative bodies to convert that into global political policy.
- Philanthropists, Global Corp's, N.G.O — These organisations and bodies take policy directives from the policy makers and distribute them to the policy enforcers.

Policy Distributers

United Nations, IMF, World Bank, I.P.C.C, W.H.O

Policy Enforcers

National Governments: Civil Service, NHS, RRU, IPSO, Ofcom, Police, Military, Courts, Local Governments, Statutory Agencies etc.

Selected Scientific Authorities: SAGE, NERVTAG, ICL, MHRA, JCVI etc.

The Policy Enforcers exploit or work with the Selected Scientific Authorities to justify the policies they are required to enforce.

Policy Propagandists

Propagandists and Hybrid Warfare Specialists: M.S.M, Fact Checkers (Politifact, Full Fact etc.), Social Media Platforms, Hybrid Warriors (77th Brigade, Huteighteen etc.), Anti-Hate Campaigners (CCE, CCDH etc)

The propagandists and hybrid warfare specialists are tasked with convincing the public to accept and hopefully believe in the policies. They use psychological manipulation, disinformation, misinformation, censorship and propaganda.

Policy Subjects

The Public

We are the subjects of the policy which cascades down through the GPP system. We largely pay for the system through taxation and public borrowing. The system is designed to exploit us but we are an increasingly unnecessary component as the GPPP look to seize the global commons.

The billionaire class must be reigned in and forced to give up much of their enormous stolen wealth. Operation Robin Hood needs to be launched on a global level to *"steal from the rich and give to the poor"* through local, national and international legal action. Everything is doable when the will of the people is activated because nothing can withstand the will of the people.

As a side-note, there is no comparison of the billionaire/trillionaire class with the average millionaire. Becoming a millionaire is a very different story. Anyone in Vancouver who owns their own home is a millionaire—the average value of a house is $1,199,400 as of October 2021. Many owners bought into the market decades ago when houses were under $300,000 and they have benefitted from the escalating real estate boom. There are several ways to become a billionaire according to Robert Reich:

1. The first way is to exploit a monopoly.
2. A second way to make a billion is to get insider information unavailable to other investors.
3. A third way to make a billion is to buy off politicians.
4. The fourth way to make a billion is to extort big investors.
5. The fifth way to be a billionaire is to get the money from rich parents or relatives.

https://www.alternet.org/2019/11/robert-reich-there-are-only-5-ways-to-become-a-billionaire-and-none-of-them-involve-being-successful-in-free-market-capitalism/

FIVE / A New Constitution

"Governments LOVE pandemics. They love pandemics for the same reason they love war. Because it gives them the ability to impose controls on the population that the population would otherwise NEVER accept."

~ Robert F. Kennedy (Berlin protest, August 29, 2020)

Let us dispense with formalities and state the obvious: Our national constitutions were not effective in preventing pharmaceutical companies, media and governments all over the world from usurping power and using the plandemic to their advantage.

Most constitutions give the government emergency powers when there is a crisis, such as war or natural disaster, but because this is such a full scale assault on the nations of the world, most constitutions were not created to prevent governments and the health authorities from abusing their powers in the current manner. Constitutional law expert Kim Lane Scheppele stated in a recent interview:

"What we're seeing is that the virus is infecting not only people and spreading but the virus has been infecting democracies that have weak or damaged constitutions. So if you have a system already in place that isn't robust, that hasn't been maintained, that has weaknesses or that has the possibility of political gaming, then the kind of extraordinary powers that somebody needs to control a pandemic are precisely the kind of powers that you see undisciplined presidents grabbing, or, weirdly, in some cases, undisciplined presidents simply letting go because they just don't seem to care about the health of the general public. The

virus actually shows which constitutions are sick, and the question is, how it is that we fix those constitutions?"

Governments in all nations struggle with their critics, naysayers, dissidents and enemies. It is normal for there to be negative public reaction to any or all of a government's policies and agendas. Every government has an agenda that they are attempting to implement and policies they want to see fulfilled—whether the government is good or bad, all governments and leaders must seek the support and gain the trust of the greatest number of people in order to maintain legitimacy as the leaders of the nation.

Our modern interconnected world has made this task much more challenging because of the complexity of our societies. The consequences of every policy decision, whether it is economic, educational, social, health related or political, has far-reaching and often unknown effects. Much of modern policy-making has been accomplished by trial-and-error.

There will always exist a tug-of-war between labor and capital, between industry and the environment, between the left and the right, between religion and science; and between nations who are competing for resources, technology and international influence.

And lastly, the global economic market is enormously affected by the stability of nations. Countries who have internal disputes and domestic problems witness a reluctance by corporations and nations to trade with them. A nation is a big machine that produces products and services that it sells and trades with other nations. Governments want their population to be good little citizens who get up every morning and go to work to keep the gears of the machine running so the nation can make money.

Nations are given credit ratings by several agencies. These ratings have a direct effect on the willingness of creditors to loan money or do business with that nation. The main rating agency is S&P (Standards and Poor) that assigns a credit score to nations based various criteria. From their website:

"*The agency has been assigning credit ratings to countries, banks, and companies since 1916. It studies the history of economic development, government reforms, the size of government debt, inflation, and the value of the national currency. It also takes into account external factors that might affect the country's economy, such as global financial crises and sanctions.*"

The top rating is AAA and there are only a handful of countries with that score: Canada, Australia, Norway, Switzerland, Germany, Denmark, Liechtenstein, Luxembourg, Netherlands and Singapore.

http://www.worldgovernmentbonds.com/world-credit-ratings/

The lowest rating is SD (Sovereign Default) and there are currently a few countries with this score: Argentina, Venezuela, Belize and Suriname. Taking the example of Venezuela whose decline has been called the worst crisis in modern history marked by hyperinflation, starvation, disease, escalating crime and mortality rates, resulting in massive emigration from the country. Inflation reached 52,000% at one point and thousands of extra-judicial assassinations against political opponents devastated the morale of the country.

https://en.wikipedia.org/wiki/Crisis_in_Venezuela#cite_note-B&C20113-16

Hunger escalated in 2016 to the point where almost seventy-five percent of the population had lost an average of over 19 lbs in weight according to this report:

https://www.upi.com/Top_News/World-News/2017/02/19/Venezuela-75-of-population-lost-19-pounds-amid-crisis/2441487523377/

Though there is not room here to discuss further, the persistent report by many trusted commentators reveals the Venezuela was systematically destroyed by the Western Elites for the refusal of former president Chavez to give into their demands. All national leaders are acutely aware of the consequences of defying the Elites. Just one article will suffice for context:

https://www.globalresearch.ca/the-destabilization-of-venezuela-applying-washington-s-benghazi-formula/27666

The point being that the Elites have enormous control over nations, and failure to submit to their demands has consequences. There is a global blanket of fear not only spread over the average citizen but it is also spread over national leaders.

We the People

What we are currently experiencing is the attempted takeover of all of our institutions by corporations and corporate owners. The misleading slogans of the Empire would have us believe these "Public-Private-Partnerships" are a sympathetic and benevolent agreement between governments and corporations. Klaus Schwab's agenda, however, is far from benevolent—it is in fact a full-court press to overthrow all democracies and install a global corporate state controlled by a handful of billionaire families and their underlings.

This is a great leap backwards on a global scale—a feudal technocracy ruled by corporate hereditary monarchs. *We the People* must rise up and destroy this Great Reset entirely. We must obliterate it and crush it to pieces with a premeditated, organized and coordinated effort of all free peoples in all nations.

During the European medieval period, the feudal system of serfs managed by the nobility and the monarchy was dominated by the totalitarian Christian Church. It became necessary to put into law the Separation of Church and State to make it illegal for the Church or any other religious institution from interfering in the political process. At the same time, democratic governments were established and civil rights and freedoms were adopted into national constitutions, guaranteeing that all people will be treated fairly and justly under the law.

This *revolution of rights* gave the people greater political autonomy that also resulted in greater economic, religious and social freedom. The people gained more power and the power of the wealthy was decreased. This is being overturned at the moment but *We the People* must fight to resist their Great Reset and restrict the power of the Elites until they are destroyed and true global democracy is created.

Who are the People?

Those of us fighting for our freedom and rights are only the spokespersons and leaders of this grand Freedom Movement that is spreading like wildfire all over our beleaguered planet. We are truly the voice of the People even though the majority of the population are brainwashed and ignorant of the reality that confronts us—we still represent their best interests.

Technically, the People are all the people of the world, but the truth is that the People are the broad mass of humanity that make up 99% of the world's population. The People are controlled by the upper 1% of the world who own and manage the vast majority of the world's wealth and resources. The 1% also are the power-holders who control governments, media, education, science, healthcare, agriculture, industry, military and just about everything else.

The 1% do not represent or speak for the People. They are concerned with their own interests and not the interests of the People. The main symptom of the world's current problems is wealth inequality. In a 2011 Vanity Fair article, economist Joseph Stiglitz commented,

"In our democracy, 1% of the people take nearly a quarter of the nation's income … In terms of wealth rather than income, the top 1% control 40% … [as a result] the top 1% have the best houses, the best educations, the best doctors, and the best lifestyles, but there is one thing that money doesn't seem to have bought: an understanding that their fate is bound up with how the other 99% live. Throughout history, this is something that the top 1% eventually do learn. Too late."

https://www.vanityfair.com/news/2011/05/top-one-percent-201105

In other words, the agenda of the Elites to bring the People to their knees will result in their own destruction.

The greater the wealth gap in a nation, the greater the level of injustice, and therefore greater systemic corruption at the highest levels of power. Wealth inequality occurs when power gets in bed with commerce. It is as simple as that. The medieval church forced the People into a situation where they had to rebel and separate from the church's control of society —separation of church and state was established. It was Thomas Jefferson who first used the phrase in a letter in 1802:

"...legislature should 'make no law respecting an establishment of religion, or prohibiting the free exercise thereof,' thus building a wall of separation between Church and State."

We the People need to establish a wall between money and politics, between Bank and State, and between private corporations and the government. Laws need to be passed and amendments to constitutions all over the world need to be put in place to restrict these nefarious Public-Private-Partnerships. The partnership between government and corporations needs to be declared null and void, the relationship terminated, the marriage annulled and the divorce made final.

Beating Swords into Plowshares

"They will beat their swords into plowshares and their spears into pruning hooks. Nation will not take up sword against nation, nor will they train for war anymore." [Isaiah 2:4]

In today's modern world, in order to fulfill this prophecy, national governments would have to melt down tanks, artillery guns, aircraft carriers and assault rifles into tractors and farming equipment. Does it seem so far-fetched that we are on the threshold of this actually happening?

Now imagine if we actually had peace on Earth and an international constitution that represented the People not the Elites. This Preamble taken from a draft of a global constitution is interesting:

PREAMBLE

We the inhabitants on planet earth, born with a supreme conscience, do hereby claim our birth right to ordain and establish universal rights and liberties, not provided for by sovereign nations. To continue our kind as limitless throughout the cosmos and beyond, we form this union to secure our bond of universal commonality.

http://globalconstitution.com/born.html#top

Or what if the United States Constitution was adopted by the entire planet? Does this seem a pipe-dream? Before the pandemic began almost two years ago it was unthinkable, but how about now? Can we see the silver lining in the horrible dark clouds:

WE THE PEOPLE of the United States of Earth, in Order to form a more perfect Union, establish Justice, insure domestic Tranquility, provide for the common defence, promote the general Welfare, and secure the Blessings of Liberty to ourselves and our Posterity, do ordain and establish this Constitution for the United States of the Earth.

SIX / Breaking Down Barriers

"We don't need no education. We don't need no thought control. No dark sarcasm in the classroom. Teacher, leave them kids alone. Hey, teachers, leave them kids alone! All in all, it's just another brick in the wall. All in all, you're just another brick in the wall."

~ *Pink Floyd, The Wall*

"Love recognizes no barriers. It jumps hurdles, leaps fences, penetrates walls to arrive at its destination full of hope."

~ *Maya Angelou*

There is good news and bad news: the good news is our Freedom Movement is dominated by conservatives. The bad news is we are all liberals. Sorry, this may come as quite a shock to many of you, but here's a towel, cry all you want. The word "liberal" comes from Latin *liber* and means "free." According to the American Heritage Dictionary definition:

Liberal: Favoring reform, open to new ideas, and tolerant of the ideas and behavior of others; not bound by traditional thinking; broad-minded.

According to history, liberalism is the political and moral philosophy born out of the Enlightenment, based on liberty, consent of the governed and equality before the law. Liberals generally support individual rights, democracy, freedom of speech, freedom of the press, freedom of religion and a free market economy. The founder of liberalism is usually identified as John Locke who argued that each person has a natural right to *life, liberty and property,* and governments must not violate these rights.

However, no one is born a liberal, conservative, libertarian or socialist. Most of us at some point in our lives, make a conscious choice to align with a particular political group. We *decide* which political or religious box we feel more comfortable in, usually in our late teens and early twenties. The majority of people follow in their parents' footsteps with regards to politics and religion, and yet still believe they have made an independent choice.

Modern psychology and neuroscience has shown that our worldview is hardwired into our brains by the time we are seven years old and that happens mostly because of the influence of our family and close community. *Like father, like son.* It takes a conscious effort to break out of the boxes we were born in.

Though it goes without saying, all human beings are biased, there are levels of bias, levels of knowledge and levels of wisdom. Wisdom comes from the ability to sort through knowledge and summarize it correctly. Some people are smarter than others, some are wiser, and some are better informed.

Knowledge can be divided into three categories:

    1. *What you know*

    2. *What you know that you don't know*

    3. *What you don't know that you don't know*

Category #3 is by far the largest category.

When we peer out of the thin atmosphere of Planet Earth into the vast unknown and view the sheer colossal size of the universe, we have a brief glimpse of how small we are relative to the rest of the universe, and we realize we are mere babes sucking at the breast of the universe—ignorant, innocent and barely awake. We are not at the end of knowledge, we are barely at the beginning.

Cognitive dissonance occurs when we are confronted with info from box #3 and reject it immediately because it destabilizes our comfort zones of box #1 and box #2, and this is mostly because human beings are afraid of the unknown.

The underlying cause of cognitive dissonance is the need for *security*. The overwhelming drive of all human behavior is not sex, money or power. It is the need for safety and security. Human beings are mammals and all mammals seek food and shelter, first and foremost. Animals need a safe place to escape the elements and protection from their enemies.

Humans also seek security and shelter within political and religious ideologies to escape the insecurities of the unknown and protect themselves from their ideological enemies. We have a basic need to find the safety and security of like-minded people—to find shelter from the storms of conflicting ideology. True freedom, however, is often the result of abandoning security in favor of the adventure of the unknown.

Coke or Pepsi

The truth is that it is not necessary to jump into any box. You can stay neutral and you will learn more. You can refuse the safety of the box and escape division. Boxes are safe and secure but true freedom means giving up on safety and security in order to learn and grow. A comfortable cage is still a cage.

You do not need to choose between Coke or Pepsi, between Democrat and Republican, between Us and Them. You are free when you *decide* to be free, and not before. The famous Chinese philosopher Confuscius said, *"The Way of Heaven does not compete, and yet it skillfully achieves victory."*

We are not here on Planet Earth to become enslaved to ideology, but rather, we are here to be set free from ideology, and thus set others free. True freedom is found by following the inner voice wherever the voice leads you. The spirit desires eternal things, seeks your spiritual growth and enlists you in the service to others above all else.

Jesus of Nazareth was the pioneer who first turned the entire notion of us-and-them upside down. He declared *"there is no Jew or Gentile, no male or female, no slave or freeman in the Kingdom of Heaven."* This was a radical message to the world order at the time and if he was here today, he might be tempted to say, *"There is no vaccinated or unvaccinated, no conservative or liberal, no Christian or non-Christian in the Kingdom of Heaven."*

In order for our Freedom Movement to conquer and destroy the false ideology of the Great Reset and the cult of fear, we must first be free ourselves. Therefore, we need to tear down barriers between all the different groups that attend our rallies. Christians, New Agers, Vegans, hippies, left and right, liberal and conservatives all need to let go of their attachment to the things that were not working before the plandemic. We can never go back to the Old Normal.

Symbolism

We're all aware of the symbols that western media is promoting constantly:

If you want further mind-boggling examples of symbolism in the media:

www.vigilantcitizen.com

https://vigilantcitizen.com/vigilantreport/the-wedding-of-billionaire-heir-ivy-getty-was-a-show-elite-power-and-symbolism/

Totalitarian regimes always employ stark symbolism to encapsulate their ideology. The current medical cult is no exception:

| Nazi Germany | Soviet Communism | Corona Fascism |

Our Freedom Movement has likewise organically employed the use of symbols to share our idealism and ideology:

FREEDOM / UNITED

VICTORY 🍁 CANADA
Let's Unite For Freedom

HUGS over MASKS.ca

NO NEW NORMAL

All social movements share an irresistible urge to represent their mission, values and goals with the use of symbols. Our movement is no exception. Symbols give people an image to easily identify with, and this is because people want to belong, and they want to live for something higher than themselves.

Animals can communicate with each other using signals and sounds, but animals have no ability to convey meanings, values and ideals. Human beings can communicate with symbols that assign and identify meanings, values, ideas and ideals.

A picture may be worth a thousands words but a symbol is worth a thousand pictures because it sums up the totality of a group, nation, cult or sub-cult. The symbol of the eagle has been used, for example by many regimes, such as the Roman Empire, Napoleon's France and the USA. The eagle symbolizes military strength, power, and freedom because the eagle can soar through the air at great heights.

Some members of the Freedom Movement complain there is too much "branding" of the different groups—we should just fight for our rights and that's it. But we are forced by the nature and global scale of the tyranny to create something new. And that means creating new symbols that can encapsulate the ideals and values of our vision of the world.

Our movement is essentially a fledgling cult—based on our civil rights, spirituality and our common philosophy of health. All religions initially began as cults that spun off from pre-existing established religions, including the early Christians who were derisively known as the "Nazarenes." Nazareth was not well-regarded by many of the conservative Jews and it gave rise to the saying *"What good can come out of Nazareth?"* This cult grew and established churches and appropriate symbolism such as the cross, the dove, the fish and many other symbols that have been employed to this day.

Our cult is slandered with labels such as "anti-vaxxers" and "anti-maskers" or "racists and white supremacists." Generally we like to be known as pro-health, vaccine-free, freedom lovers, truthers or collectively *The Freedom Movement*. If we wanted to be more accurate we could say we are an international movement fighting for civil rights, health autonomy and the restoration of justice, democracy and spirituality.

Ecumenicalism

Absolute truth is indestructible. Being indestructible, it is eternal. Being eternal, it is self-existent. Being self-existent, it is infinite. Being infinite, it is vast and deep. Being vast and deep, it is transcendental and intelligent. It is because it is vast and deep that it contains all existence. It is because it is transcendental and intelligent that it embraces all existence. It is because it is infinite and eternal that it fulfills or perfects all existence. In vastness and depth it is like the Earth. In transcendental intelligence it is like Heaven. Infinite and eternal, it is the Infinite itself. Such being the nature of absolute truth, it manifests itself without being seen; it produces effects without motion; it accomplishes its ends without action.

~ Confucianism. Doctrine of the Mean 26

Many in our Freedom Movement contend that the Elites want a one-world religion, though it seems what they are doing is attempting is to destroy all religion. The history of totalitarian regimes like Stalinist Russia,

Maoist China and Nazi Germany records a definite historical pattern of systematic efforts to eradicate religion from society.

It is not possible for the world's religions to unite because they just have too many ideological obstacles that cannot be overcome at this time. However, our movement can become the catalyst for interfaith dialogue and create the space for the world's religions to find common ground and lessen tensions. The road to peace is paved with communication and openness.

As a side-note, the word ecumenical comes from the Latin word *oecumenicus* which means *general* or *universal*. The only way to have a universal faith is to have universal principles that we can all agree on. All religions teach better relationships between families, friends and nations. Whether they practice what they preach is another subject but there is still more commonality with world religions than differences. Every religion has some expression of the Golden Rule:

Whatever you wish that men would do to you, do so to them.

~ Christianity. Bible, Matthew 7.12

Not one of you is a believer until he loves for his brother what he loves for himself.

~ Islam. Forty Hadith of an-Nawawi 13

A man should wander about treating all creatures as he himself would be treated.

~ Jainism. Sutrakritanga 1.11.33

Try your best to treat others as you would wish to be treated yourself, and you will find that this is the shortest way to benevolence.

~ Confucianism. Mencius VII.A.4

One should not behave towards others in a way which is disagreeable to oneself. This is the essence of morality. All other activities are due to selfish desire.

~ Hinduism, Mahabharata, Anusasana Parva 113.8

Ayyavazhi	Bahai	Buddhism	Christianity *Latin cross*	Christianity *Greek cross*
Christianity *Orthodox cross*	Christianity *Chi-Rho/Labarum*	Christianity *JHS Christogram*	Christianity *Ichthys*	Hinduism
Islam	Jainism	Jainism	Judaism	Paganism
Paganism	Paganism	Sikhism	Shinto	Taoism

All religions have commandments prohibiting murder, stealing, lying, and adultery. All religions teach peace, love and wisdom. If we want to create a more peaceful world, we all have to learn to embrace the best in each other, the best in other cultures and the best in other religions. And at the same time, distancing ourselves from the negative things that have proven again and again throughout history to lead to death and destruction.

Reverse Tower of Babel

Our world has 194 countries with different religions, cultures, political systems and languages. We cannot hope to suddenly turn the whole planet into a homogenous blob of culture and language, though it actually seems this is what the Empire of Chaos is trying to achieve; an impossible task doomed to disaster.

Their symbol of the monolithic four-sided tower actually represent a reverse Tower of Babel, attempting to merge all cultures and religions under a single symbol. Sightings of simple metal monoliths suddenly appeared all over the world in 2020. Whether these are more predictive programming of the Elites is a matter of conjecture but usually these strange happenings have the Elites' fingerprints all over them: *https://www.insider.com/at-least-87-monoliths-have-appeared-worldwide-since-utah-2020-12*

Monolith appeared in East Vancouver Dec. 2020

SEVEN / Cats & Dogs

Our Freedom Movement talks a lot about sheep, usually in a disparaging tone referring to the poor brainwashed sheep who believe everything they are told by the media, and do whatever they are told by our government and demented health officials. So sad, too bad.

The carpenter's son from Nazareth also talked about sheep on several occasions. The parable of the lost sheep is a bitter irony today, because if Jesus were here he would have to contend with a hundred lost sheep instead of just one.

If you've ever spent any time on a farm you know that sheep are very trusting and naive, right up until they are slaughtered—but this chapter isn't about sheep—it's about cats and dogs, and the differences between them. Cats are very independent and seem to tolerate human beings more than love them. They can go off on their own for days and then come back for a bite to eat and a nap, and then go back out again.

Our Freedom Movement, for better or worse, is dominated by cats and as the saying goes, you can't herd cats. Another piece of wisdom: we can't win a war with a herd of cats. An army could never hope to win at anything if it was an army of cats. Neither would the police ever be able to train a police-cat.

We need dogs. Dogs are loyal, obedient and protective. They are called man's best friend and rightly so—they would die for their owners if needed. Dogs are teachable, trainable, trustworthy and easy to work with. They are cheerful servants.

There are many freedom fighters in our movement who have the dog-spirit and in the long run, they will undoubtedly dominate our movement. And that is not to say that there is anything wrong with being independent, self-reliant and aloof. The libertarian streak that runs through our movement gives us strength but it needs to be tempered with the spirit that allows us to bond together and work together as a team. Without teamwork in this war, we are doomed.

Teamwork

"Teamwork is the ability to work together toward a common vision, the ability to direct individual accomplishments toward organizational objectives. It is the fuel that allows common people to attain uncommon results."

~ Andrew Carnegie

According to Richard Hackman, a Harvard professor of organizational psychology, and a leading expert on teams, small teams can generate magic but it's not guaranteed. The belief that teams make us more creative and productive—and are the best way to get things done—is deeply entrenched. Often teams underperform despite all their extra resources because of several common mistakes that renders them ineffective.

The biggest pitfall is that members often do not agree on what the team is supposed to be doing or even on who is on the team. Without a clearly stated and agreed-upon goal, your Freedom Cell will accomplish little, other than getting together and offering moral support to each other.

Bigger is not always better and as a team grows, the effort needed to manage the members increases almost exponentially. If your group becomes too big, the ideal plan is to split it into two groups.

The leader of the cell group needs to be ruthless about defining teams and keeping them small (fewer than 10 members). Negative individuals can be team destroyers and they should simply be forced out of the group. The leader also must set a compelling direction for the team—but in so doing, may encounter intense resistance that puts the whole group at risk, and it could fall apart if there is too much dispute over the direction and goals of the team.

Another fallacy about teams is that those with long-term membership eventually become stale. In fact, Hackman's research reveals that new teams make 50% more mistakes than established teams. The group must be patient and allow for sufficient time for everyone to gel. Give yourselves at least a year, because just like wine, it gets better with age.

Every team needs a deviant to avoid complacency—someone who is willing to stir up enough debate and dissension to open up the group to new ideas. Unfortunately, such individuals often get thrown off the team, robbing it of its chance to be magical. The leader needs to discern whether the individual is a destroyer or a deviant.

No matter how good the leader is, he or she cannot force the team to perform. However, by being disciplined about how a team is set up and managed, instituting the right support systems, and providing coaching in group processes, the leader can increase the likelihood that a team will be great.

The most important meeting is the first meeting. Generally, small groups establish everything in the first moments, including the goals, direction, structure and group dynamics. The team leader needs to be very conscious of this fact and be quick to steer the first meeting carefully and competently.

One of the other fallacies of small teams is that they have to be running harmoniously to function properly. The reality is that the team needs to have some tension to keep it vital and effective. Too much tension, however is bad and the team may fall apart if there is excessive social drama. It's usually the leader's job to maintain the balance, although the group may need a peace-maker—someone who helps smooth out the rough edges between members.

https://obmi.institute/lekce/7-hackmans-five-factors-model/

Individualism vs Collectivism

Our international battle to regain our civil rights, restore democracy and push back the overwhelming tyranny that has engulfed the world is seasoned by the salt of our charters of rights and freedoms that were achieved through decades, even centuries of struggle. The horrifying truth is that these rights and freedoms vanished overnight in the early days of the plandemic of March 2020.

A magic spell descended over the world and our governments and their citizens drank deeply of the Covid Kool-aid. In Donald's Trump address to the

American people in July, 2020 he mocked the tragedy in the darkest tones:

"So think of it, in this horrible period, this horrible, horrible dark period, where a monster came and worked its horrible, horrible spell over the world."

How dare these willful, selfish miscreants deprive the entire world of the right to live freely. Our basic human rights are for the best interests of all citizens and our world leaders are blatantly taking advantage of the goodwill of average citizens, coercing and manipulating them through psychological torture and playing on their innocent desire to do what is best for the community.

| Key Differences Between Individualist and Collectivist Societies ||
Individualist	Collectivist
Everyone grows up to look after him/herself and his/her immediate family only.	People are born into extended families or in other groups that continue protecting them in exchange for loyalty.
Children learn to think in terms of "I".	Children learn to think in terms of "we".
Individual ownership of resources.	Resources should be shared with relatives.
Low-context communication prevails.	High context communication prevails.
Media is the primary source of information.	Social networks are the primary source of information.
Self-actualization by every individual is a ultimate goal.	Harmony and consensus in society are ultimate goal.
Occupation mobility is higher.	Occupation mobility is lower.
Task prevails over relationship.	Relationship prevails over task.
Individual interests prevail over collective.	Collective interest prevail over individual.
Per capita GDP tends to be higher.	Per capital GDP tends to be lower.

Rights are extended not only to the individual but also to the collective. An individual does not have the right to exercise his or her freewill if their actions harm or infringe on the rights of others, so there is always a balance between retaining our personal autonomy and protecting the rights of the group.

True liberty sets everyone free.

A nation has a right to create laws and enforce those laws through a police department. It has the right to create an army, build roads and infrastructure by virtue of the mandate granted to them by the people, assuming the nation is a democracy. Even undemocratic nations gain their right to authority through constitutions and rights granted by agreement of the ruling body.

Our movement cannot be so anarchist or libertarian to ignore the rights of our governments, families and communities. It is doubtful a family could be raised on anarchy. Should the child say to the parents that the parent's authority is an infringement on his rights? The reaction to totalitarian regimes should never be to abolish all government. What we need is good government run by competent men and women with the best interests of the people at heart, and with the foresight and ability to enact long-term policies that are for the greater good.

EIGHT / A World United

Any discussion of the United Nations is bound to be a thorny one for the majority of people in the Freedom Movement. The Elites' plans for world government includes using the United Nations as leverage to further the Sustainable Development Goals and Agenda 2030. There are, of course, many other institutions they either control or have influence over that they are manipulating to achieve their goal of global domination. A brief list of these organizations would have to include the World Bank, the WHO, the IMF, the BIS, Wall Street and the City of London. Other groups include the World Economic Forum, the Bilderberg group, the Council of Foreign Relations, the Trilateral Commission and the newly formed Quadilateral Security Dialogue (2007).

https://en.wikipedia.org/wiki/Quadrilateral_Security_Dialogue

The League of Nations was the first international step towards a world government and the United Nations is its natural heir. It is no small task to convince 193 nations to give up their sovereignty and hand it over to a world government, especially when it is visibly obvious to all national leaders that the western oligarchs dominate the institution and they are not interested in democracy.

Non-Aligned Movement

There are other international think tanks that many are unaware of, such as the Non-Aligned Movement that was established in 1961 in Belgrade, Yugoslavia through an initiative of the Indian Prime Minister

Jawaharlal Nehru, Yugoslav President Josip Broz Tito, Egyptian President Gamal Abdel Nasser, Ghanaian President Kwame Nkrumah and Indonesian President Sukarno. The NAM currently represents 120 nations, virtually all of them are members of the Global South of developing nations—the have-nots, in other words.

The Non-Aligned Movement was created as a reaction against the Cold War division between USA and the USSR and their respective allies. The NAM has been calling for decades for reform of the United Nations, especially reform of the UN Security Council which is representative of the world order after WW2 when the five victor nations of USA, UK, France, China and Russia (who are all nuclear powers incidentally) were given veto power.

https://en.wikipedia.org/wiki/Non-Aligned_Movement

The addition of Brazil, Germany, India, and Japan as permanent members of the UN Security Council has been floated since 1992 with varying degrees of support and opposition. The 54 African nations have also endorsed making two African nations permanent security council members.

Here is one of the most scathing comments of the UNSC by international journalist and UN civil servant Erskine Barton Childers: *"the vast majority of members – North as well as South – have made very clear...their distaste for the way three Western powers [UK, US, and France] behave in the Council, like a private club of hereditary elite-members who secretly come to decisions and then emerge to tell the grubby elected members that they may now rubber-stamp those decisions."*

The UN for decades has been following the World Economic Forum's "stakeholder capitalist" model (created by Klaus Schwab) that favors the private sector and billionaire "philanthropists" over national governments, with the latter delegated with creating "enabling environments" for the policies that benefit the billionaire class.

Speaking to the World Economic Forum in 1998, Secretary General Kofi Annan outlined this fundamental shift explicitly, calling it a quiet revolution:

"The United Nations has been transformed since we last met here in Davos. The Organization has undergone a complete overhaul that I have described as a 'quiet revolution.'"...A fundamental shift has occurred. The United Nations once dealt only with governments. By now we know that peace and prosperity cannot be achieved without partnerships involving governments, international organizations, the business community and civil society...The business of the United Nations involves the businesses of the world."

The critics of the United Nation vary in their opinions, from dissolving the UN all together, to those on the other side of the argument who are pushing for making the UN the official world government. Before tackling this issue, it is important to point out that one of the cornerstones of the UN Charter is the Universal Declarations of Human Rights, a document initiated by Elenor Roosevelt and authored by Canadian legal scholar, John Peters Humphrey. Along with the creation of the UN came an advance in universal human rights, proving that any institution can be a force for good or evil, depending on the institutional owners.

The United Nations is not a world government (yet.) It lacks the division of powers of executive, legislative and judicial branches, though the UNSC functions somewhat as an executive committee. It does not collect taxes nor does it have a standing army—the UN blue helmets operate on a case-by-case method, creating an ad hoc force as needed per mission. The UN is basically an international public forum that has limited powers to intervene in small local wars and acts primarily as a global advisory panel. This may, however change very rapidly in the near future if the Empire of Chaos gets its way.

The African Union

The idea of a continental union of 55 African states was promoted in the 1990's by Muammar Gaddafi who dominated the movement up until his death in 2011. The Organisation of African Unity was officially declared on 9 September 1999 with the Sirte Declaration, named after the location of the conference in Sirte, Libya. This was followed a year letter by 53 states signing a constitution:

https://au.int/sites/default/files/treaties/7758-treaty-0021_-_constitutive_act_of_the_african_union_e.pdf

Before his death Gaddafi pushed hard for a United States of Africa, and in February 2009, upon being elected chairman of the 53-nation African Union in Ethiopia, Gaddafi told the assembled African leaders: "I shall continue to insist that our sovereign countries work to achieve the United States of Africa," and further proposed "a single African military force, a single currency and a single passport for Africans to move freely around the continent."

According to their website the African Union has a 50-year plan known as Agenda 2063:

"As an affirmation of their commitment to support Africa's new path for attaining inclusive and sustainable economic growth and development African heads of state and government signed the 50th Anniversary Solemn Declaration during the Golden Jubilee celebrations of the formation of the OAU/AU in May 2013. The declaration marked the re-dedication of Africa towards the attainment of the Pan African Vision of an integrated, prosperous and peaceful Africa, driven by its own citizens, representing a dynamic force in the international arena."

UNASUR and PROSUR

A group of South American presidents met in March of 2019 to launch a new regional bloc to replace the Union of South American Nations (UNASUR) that was promoted by Venezuelan President Hugo Chavez to counter U.S. influence in the region.

The previous group, called UNASUR, was started in 2008 when most of the originating nations were governed by leftist governments but enthusiasm dwindled as more conservative and moderate governments emerged. "UNASUR is a wonderful opportunity we have today to consolidate South America as a zone of democratic peace...that is our armour against barbarism...it is the most reliable guarantee that providence can give us so that we can assure the continuity of our republics and South American independence," said Chávez.

Eventually, the 12 nations suspended their memberships over leadership differences and partly for UNASUR's failure to take action in crisis-torn Venezuela. Chilean Foreign Minister Roberto Ampuero stated that the organization "isn't getting anywhere, there is no integration" and that "We can't be throwing this money to an institution that doesn't work."

Leaders of the PROSUR (Forum for the Progress and Development of South America) bloc launched in the Chilean capital of Santiago said the new group will focus on defending democracy and freedom. In their joint declaration, they committed to "renew and strengthen" regional integration under a more flexible and effective framework. The founding presidents of PROSUR are from Argentina, Brazil, Chile, Colombia, Ecuador, Paraguay and Peru.

Venezuelan President Hugo Chávez with UNASUR Secretary General María Enma Mejía (AVN).

The BRICS and the New Silk Roads

Another global game-changer that involves a multitude of nations is the Belt and Road Initiative, commonly know New Silk Roads project, that is promoted, funded and organized by China in cooperation with the BRICS (Brazil, Russia, India, China, South Africa). Just as a side-note to avoid confusion: the author is in no way advocating or endorsing communism or the CCP. The New Silk Roads is an infrastructure project, not a political ideology.

China is currently offering almost a trillion dollars in loans to 68 countries to create roads, rail, new ports and telecommunication networks spanning the breadth of Eurasia. This is without a doubt the largest infrastructure project in world history. Ironically, one of the more lucid articles on the subject is on the World Economic Forum's website:

https://www.weforum.org/agenda/2017/06/china-new-silk-road-explainer/

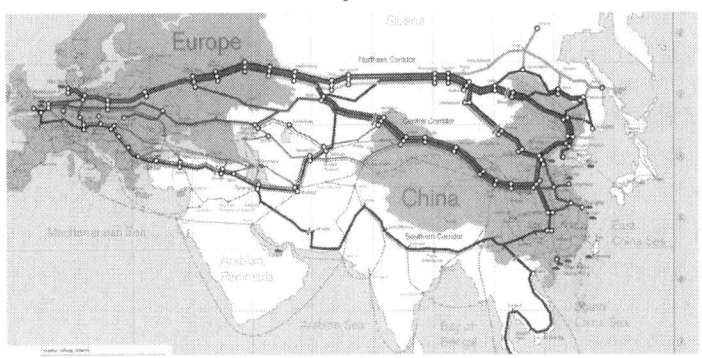

Are the Western Elites involved in this plan for some nefarious agenda? Considering the current US-China trade war and sanctions initiated by the US, it would seems unlikely, yet these are not normal times.

The Multi-Polar World Order

"Russia is in favor of a multipolar world, a democratic world order, strengthening the system of international law, and for developing a legal system in which any small country, even a very small country, can feel itself secure, as if behind a stone wall."

~ *Vladimir Putin*

The majority of people in the Freedom Movement are adamantly opposed to the idea of an actual United Nations or, in other words, a one-world government for three main reasons: First, the assumption that a one-world government would automatically be a tyranny.

Secondly, because the Elites are pushing for it, that must mean it's a bad idea. And lastly, because of Christian end-times prophecies that are being interpreted in the context of today's events.

How is all of this relevant to our goal of creating a better world? The short version is that unless our Freedom Movement develops and grows to a size that has the political and social clout to impact the United Nations, we are probably not going to be successful in many of our long-term goals.

The same can be said of any negotiations with the Non-Aligned Movement. We may, in fact have better luck in developing dialogue with the NAM than with the UN because they are, by default, at odds with the established world order and we may get a more sympathetic audience with them.

There are also a multitude of other international organizations that we can appeal to and attempt to form alliances, build bridges and open up dialogue. The issues brought out into the open by the pandemic have made it imperative that we take our cause to the highest levels of the global community. We have no other choice.

Though it is far beyond the scope of this brief book to fully detail the global situation, the short version of the current state of affairs on the international scene is a struggle between the Western Empire of Chaos and the rest of the world who do not want to be under their boot. Nations like China, Russia, Iran, and many others want an international system based on law and not the "rules-based order" that the NWO is advocating. This is further complicated by the fact that

Russia and China are in bed economically with the West and as the saying goes, *if you make your bed you have to lie in it.*

The rules-based order is like Facebook's Community Standards: arbitrary rules that are enforced without any discussion or appeal. The United States and its NATO allies are, at the time of this writing, confronting Russia over the Ukraine, confronting China over Taiwan and the South China Sea and carrying on with their hybrid war of CIA espionage, intrigue and aggression against a multitude of nations.

Nations who refuse to submit to the United States are sanctioned, such as the 50-year embargo against Cuba. Sanctions are financial warfare and they are exceedingly damaging to a nation's economy and development. What all nations want is to retain their sovereignty. They give up sovereignty to the United States and the New World Order through coercion, bombing campaigns, invasion, or through fake coups orchestrated by the NWO and their various agents—the CIA being the most glaring example.

The Multi-Polar World Order is however also a dangerous proposition because it forces all 193 UN nations into a balance-of-power arrangement like the European history of alliances in the medieval period that resulted in continual war and conflict. Any basic study of European history reveals a tangled web of ever-changing alliances, betrayals, broken treaties, and endless wars.

https://www.strategic-culture.org/news/2016/08/20/multipolar-world-order-economics-vs-politics/

Finally, the most painful truth is that it appears that, despite the antagonism between Russia, China and the United States, both Russia and China have partnered with the West to push the coronavirus nightmare. Recent reports out of Russia are verifying the Sputnik V vaccine is also a gene-altering product that is having all kinds of adverse effects.

https://edwardslavsquat.substack.com/p/sputnik-v-is-a-scam

And if you have a strong stomach, check out this Twitter account about the current nightmare in China: *Viewer Discretion Advised*

https://twitter.com/songpinganq

Double-Edged Sword

Nationalism is a double-edged sword: One side of the blade keeps the NWO in check because nations do not want to hand over their sovereignty to global psychopaths; and the other side of the blade strikes at the heart of any attempts to create a global system of law and order.

We can't have our cake and eat it too. We cannot create global peace if nations are at odds with each other, suspicious of each other and competing with each other over land and resources. We do not want a forced phony peace of totalitarian control either.

In 1950, James Warburg, the son of one of the Council on Foreign Relations' founders, David Warburg, arrogantly proclaimed to the Senate Foreign Relations Committee:

"We shall have world government whether or not you like it – by conquest or consent."

The truth is that he was right. The globalist elites are attempting to install a one world government by *conquest* because the world will never voluntarily agree to their totalitarian system. The plandemic of media propaganda is their final push to conquer the world.

The United States was a union of thirteen colonies who gave up their sovereignty in order to form "a more perfect union." Likewise, the EU nations gave up sovereignty to form the European Union. There has been peace in Europe since World War Two when the European Economic Community of six nations was born.

Although, it is highly probable that any discussion of a one world government, even a democratic one, will elicit groans of protest from our Freedom Movement, the seeds of a global democracy were already planted centuries ago. The Elites did not invent the idea of a global government. All they have done is run to the front of the parade in the vain attempt to usurp control of the natural political evolution of our planet. They want to shortcut this process and accelerate the natural evolution of world affairs. Is it any wonder, the vaccine rollout is called Operation Warpspeed? If left alone, it may take hundreds of years before our world is ready for a peaceful global alliance of nations.

The Elites do not want one world *government*; what they want is corporate *governance*—a hereditary monarchy who run the world through a corporate board of directors that manage feudal slaves through technology, artificial intelligence and surveillance.

The Multi-Polar World Order advocated by many leaders on the international stage may eventually morph into a global government by *consent* of all nations. Furthermore, the plans of the Elites for a totalitarian world Empire will fail. That is the real future.

BASIC PRINCIPLES OF WORLD GOVERNMENT

[excerpted from "World Government via the United Nations" by Clark M. Eichelberger, 1949]

Those who believe in world government want essentially a few definite things.

First, the law of the world community must be above the sovereignty of the individual nation. There must be a supreme law against war.

Second, there must be an executive authority strong enough to use police force or whatever measures are necessary to preserve the peace.

Third, there must be a constant procedure for producing such regulations as are necessary to lessen friction among the peoples of the world and enable them to grow and expand in their world community. It might be called the legislative process.

And above everything else there must be a sense on the part of the peoples of the world that they are members of a common society with common objectives and ideals toward world peace, toward economic advancement, and toward respect for human rights and the dignity of the individual.

https://journals.sagepub.com/doi/pdf/10.1177/000271624926400105

The Sky is Falling

Our society has become corrupt, not only at the core of the Deep State, but also the People are corrupted. Pornography is rampant, sex trafficking, and pedophilia are normalized. Unbridled self-gratification is the sure death of any civilization. Without divine intervention, the West is doomed. Incidentally, there is no record of divine intervention that halted the fall of the Roman Empire. If Christianity could not save the Roman Empire, then judging by the apathy of the churches at this time of crisis, it is highly unlikely that Christianity can save the American Empire. The good news is that it does not mean that Canada or America are lost. The Roman Empire fell but Italy carried on. The Greek Empire fell but we still have Greece.

Even a good religion can not save a nation or empire from the certain results from lack of individual participation in the affairs of government. We can blame the Elites for everything but it is the People who created the power vacuum that allowed the sociopaths to become entrenched in all facets of our society. It has taken them decades to get this level of control of media, medicine, government, education and the economy. We the People need to return to public involvement in the political arena. It is that simple.

NINE / The Resistance

"Cautious, careful people, always casting about to preserve their reputation and social standing, never can bring about a reform. Those who are really in earnest must be willing to be anything or nothing in the world's estimation, and publicly and privately, in season and out, avow their sympathy with despised and persecuted ideas and their advocates, and bear the consequences."
~ Susan B. Anthony, 1860

The world will not be changed by complacent sheep who fear the wolves. The universe favors the bold. Even evil men accomplish little unless they are aggressive, organized and make radical plans that challenge the status quo. The amount of planning and coordination of this staged plandemic is ample proof of the organizational skills of our enemies.

Small men and women with small ideas make small plans and accomplish little. Our plans must be extraordinary, our resolve absolute, and our victory complete. We can accept nothing less than the complete overthrow of the Empire of Secular Materialism.

The plandemic has awoken the sleeping giant. We must become the Elites' worst nightmare and unleash the full weight of the people's will upon them. The general rule of the universe is that slow evolution wins the day; violent revolution often results in a worse situation so we must be diligent to manage our movement lest it slide into a global civil war. Unfortunately, this may happen anyway as the cauldron of simmering anger and frustration boils over.

Rick Thomas

Recruiting the Neutrals

In every country on Earth, there are certain dynamics that always apply. There is an established government in power and an elected or unelected opposition that is dissatisfied with the ruling regime and wants reform and attempts to oust the established rulers and install their own group.

Elections follow a similar pattern: 30-40% of the electorate vote conservative every election no matter what; and 30-40% of the electorate vote liberal every election, no matter what. The remaining 20-40% of the population are the neutral swing-voters. Elections are invariably decided by neutrals who bounce back and forth between opposing forces.

Our current gang of tyrants gained support from the population through media propaganda, coercion from health officials and the complicit support of corporations and institutions. The people were terrorized and lied to, and then forced to obey the new mandates or risk losing their jobs and face being banned from restaurants, concerts and events.

Our Freedom Movement represents the percentage of the population that are either actively or passively opposed to this, even though many have complied because they see no other alternative. Our movement must provide an alternative plan in order for the neutrals to swing their support our way. The neutrals haven't really looked carefully at the available data; they are just going along with things because they are either not that concerned, they assume things will eventually go back to normal or they felt they had no choice because the alternative of losing their jobs, careers, homes and families was far too terrible.

This does not leave them off the hook however. Anyone who has taken the jab effectively supports the policies of our government and health officials.

Many of these are among the apolitical youth who just want to go to night clubs, and restaurants and hang out with their friends. All the universities are forcing our youth to be vaccinated or face suspension from school.

Our movement started with the older population of over 40-year olds, but the youth are beginning to wake up. Traditionally, activism and dissent comes from the intelligentsia of university-educated youth. Winning the youth to our side would be an enormous, if not, decisive victory.

Those who have lost their jobs because they refused the jab will be looking for us to plug in and fight back. Same with the small businesses who will continue to face extinction as the corporate monsters roll out their Great Reset. They will come to us and we need to be ready for them.

The other group of neutrals will come from those who were injured from the mRNA injections or had friends and family members injured or killed from the vaxx. They will wake up the hard way and begin posting on social media about their injured relatives. This has already started happening.

The strategy of forming small autonomous groups is the best way of getting the neutrals plugged into our movement. These cliques of freedom fighters can be either formal weekly meetings or just informal circles of friends. The neutrals will come to the rallies and look for information and moral support. People join political/social movements because of their ideological stance but they stay because of the relationships they form with fellow activists.

The sociopathic Elites want the people isolated, masked and brainwashed. They want to squash freedom of speech, freedom of press and freedom of association in order to create a compliant, docile population but we can form close-knit communities and re-create the pioneer-spirit that first began here in Canada and the United States in the 1600's.

Victimizers

A skillful psychological manipulator victimizes others in a subtle way that doesn't appear obvious to outsiders. Those who have experienced psychological bullying understand that the abuser claims innocence because the abuse is covert not overt and therefore difficult to prove.

The elites are using the same tactic of deflecting blame and creating a social scapegoat out of the unvaccinated population and turning the vaccinated people against them. These are basic tactics of fascism put into practice by the Nazi government in World War II who blamed the Jews for all the problems of Germany.

Because of the record of history we are forewarned of their tactics. The Jews in Nazi Germany didn't know what was coming. When they were forced into ghettos and then herded onto trains that took them to concentration camps they had no idea what the their fate would be.

A recent letter from survivors of the holocaust begins:

"We, the survivors of the atrocities committed against humanity during the Second World War, feel bound to follow our conscience and write this letter.

It is obvious to us that another holocaust of greater magnitude is taking place before our eyes. The majority of the world's populace do not yet realize what is happening, for magnitude of an organized crime such as this is beyond their scope of experience.

We, however, know. We remember the name Josef Mengele. Some of us have personal memories. We experience a déjà vu that is so horrifying that we rise to shield our poor fellow humans. The threatened innocents now include children, and even infant.

In just four months, the COVID-19 vaccines have killed more people than all available vaccines combined from mid-1997 until the end of 2013—a period of 15.5 years. And people affected worst are between 18 and 64 years old – the group which was not in the Covid statistics.

We call upon you to stop this ungodly medical experiment on humankind immediately."

https://www.globalresearch.ca/stop-the-covid-holocaust-open-letter/5755902

Third World War

We are in a war and the reason we know there is a war is because people are being killed by an organized enemy. If nobody is dying, then there is no war.

There were only six countries who openly opposed the WHO healthcare mandates: Burundi, Swaziland, Tanzania, Ivory Coast, Haiti and Belarus, and the leaders are all dead now, except Lukashenko from Belarus, who on August 12, 2021, stated that he is strongly opposed to making vaccination mandatory:

"There will be no mandatory vaccination in Belarus. I am strongly against it. Vaccination will remain voluntary. If a person wants to be vaccinated it is good, if not, let it be."

It would not be fair to take wagers on his life expectancy at this point.

Murder by Government

Persons Killed In The Twentieth Century, By Cause		
Cause	Total (Millions)	Average per 100,000 Population
Government Non-War (all)	119.4	349
Communist	95.2	477
Other non-free	20.3	495
Partially free	3.1	48
Free	.8	22
War (all)	35.7	22
International	29.7	17
Civil	6.0	26

According to extensive study of wartime and peacetime deaths by government action done by Professor Rudolph J. Rummel of the University of Hawaii, deaths at the hands of government in peacetime totaled more than three times as many deaths deaths during wartime. The conclusion of the last 100 years is that the enemy has become our governments and now we are faced with the reality that the dictatorial police state is now emerging as a *global* police state.

Professor Rummel invented the term *democide* for *murder by government*, such as the genocide of indigenous peoples, colonialism, Nazi Germany, the Stalinist purges, Mao Zedong's Cultural Revolution, and other authoritarian, totalitarian, or undemocratic regimes. His study concluded that democratic regimes result in the least democides. Rummel found that there were 205 wars between non-democracies, 166 wars between non-democracies and democracies, and no wars between democracies during the period between 1816 and 2005.

https://en.wikipedia.org/wiki/Rudolph_Rummel

Democratic governments are the result of ideals of freedom and equality that have developed over the last few centuries. These ideals are primarily based on the unconscious acceptance and influence of the teachings of Jesus of Nazareth whose ideas on spirituality were inseparable from his views on equality, justice and a compassionate society.

TEN / The New Spiritualists

Global Death Cult

It may be stating the obvious but the Christian Church in North America and Europe has failed to be the Salt of the Earth during the plandemic—the salt has lost its savor. The same can be said of all the major world religions. The Tibetan leader, the Dalai Lama was one of the first to be vaccinated when the mRNA injections rolled out in January 2021. "This is very very helpful, very good," he said as he was given the Oxford-AstraZeneca jab at a facility in the Indian city of Dharamsala in March, 2021.

"Thanks to God's grace and to the work of many, we now have vaccines to protect us from Covid-19," Pope Francis is on record as saying, "It's an act of love."

Echoing the Pope in lockstep are a long list of religious leaders advocating we inject our bodies with toxic chemicals. Rabbi Shmuel Herzfeld of Ohev Sholom synagogue in Washington, DC, rolled up his holy robe last July and volunteered to have his DNA modified with Moderna's lethal injection. Herzfeld received a medical hero award for his service to the Empire of Death.

"Saving lives is an act of worship" leading Tahirul Qadri scholar urged Muslims to have COVID vaccine. Maybe if you're worshipping Satan, it's an act of worship. He claimed, "Vaccine conspiracy theories go against the tenets of Islam."

Vaxx-pushing Pastor Franklin Graham developed pericarditis after getting jabbed but still claimed "if there were vaccines available in the time of Christ, Jesus would have made reference to them and used them." We can only imagine the sermon: *"Blessed are the vaccinated for they shall be allowed in night clubs."*

[CNN broadcast screenshot: "RACE TO VACCINATE — GRAHAM URGES EVANGELICALS TO GET VACCINE BEFORE 'IT'S TOO LATE'", Boone, NC, 8:29 AM ET]

On April 2, 2021, in Britain, the Sikh community decided the best way to celebrate the upcoming holy festival of Vaisakhi was with a vaccination clinic. "Vaisakhi is all about Sikhs carrying out selfless service, and what better selfless service than opening up a pop-up clinic that reaches out to anybody of any religion," said Randhawa, one of the organizers or the event. "So today, we have got people from the Muslim faith, the Christian faith, Sikhs, all coming in to be vaccinated."

Depending on how far down the rabbit hole you want to go, we might be tempted to speculate that our global religious leaders are just as corrupt and paid-for as our leaders, media and health officials. There is no reason to conclude otherwise. The most hopeful thing we could say is they are brainwashed kool-aid drinkers who have join the global death cult.

The Non-Affiliated Community

If the churches, temples, synagogues and mosques have failed at this time of crisis, then what should we do? Boycott them? Or just start new churches, temples, synagogues and mosques?

Or the other alternative is to do neither, and instead plant the seeds of a new way of doing religion that doesn't segregate people into denominations and dogmas. We can all come together in a spirit of unity without advocating a creed, cult or mandate. The proof is at many of the rallies, events, workshops and meetings we have hosted here in Vancouver, with people of all faiths joining hands in brotherhood and sisterhood, sharing the same spirit, drinking from the same well.

We are joined together in the spirit when we do the things the spirit wills. Spiritual unity happens organically whenever we do the spirit things together. *Where two or three are gathered together, there will my spirit be.* The byproduct of doing these spiritual goals is we form a spiritual brotherhood and sisterhood.

Religious organizations require a building, a priest-class and a set of doctrines that they all share. Spiritual brotherhood only requires willing hearts working together, with or without buildings, a priest-class or set of doctrines. The spirit doesn't need us all to agree on everything. Our spiritual parent, guardian, Great

Spirit, Higher Power, Universal Father, Mother of All only looks for willing hands and hearts.

Meditation, Creation, Affection, Devotion

The beauty of meditating together with a group of people is the silence created. Silence is the canvas that the inner spirit speaks to us on. Meditation is one of the most accessible group activities for spiritual people. Communion, prayer, worship, song and dance are also universal with all religions. Simply holding hands in a circle is a spiritual experience.

Drawing together in silence helps unite us, especially outside in nature where we are closer to creation. We all come from nature, our bodies are born from the Earth and or bodies return to the Earth when we pass from this Earth to the next world.

Ashes to ashes, dust to dust.

Human beings, like all warm-blooded animals, need affection. Baby dolphins, elephants, bears, dogs, cats, lions and primates need their mother's love to survive and thrive. This never ends. We always need hugs and the human touch from womb to tomb.

The Elites' psychopathic attempt to destroy human connection and affection will prove to be an abject failure. They may be master psychologists and shrewd manipulators but we see through their strategy. Torturing the human race with lockdowns, plagues and isolation may temporarily traumatize us but we will bounce back. Their psycho-voodoo, like a magic spell, will eventually wear off.

And furthermore, all their plans will die like weeds without water. They will only heighten and highlight the need for human affection. The human race will be even stronger and more devoted to each other in the future. It's already happening. They have inadvertently created our Freedom Family because of their evil intentions, and this same family, who are the true Salt of the Earth, will pour salt on their wounds while their plans fall apart and their Empire crumbles.

Connecting to Source

We're all spiritual beings, but we have different backgrounds and approaches to spirituality. Some are more inclined to organized religion, others to a purely personal and private religion. One of the key differences is whether or not we refer to the Source as a who or a what. Whether you view the Source as a personality or an energy source or a cosmic mind still leaves you with the freedom to connect to the Source.

When we are together fighting for our freedom we should all be united by the spirit in our meetings, rallies and events—the Spirit of Freedom. Many are calling their small cell groups *"Freedom Circles"* and joining hands together in a circle. Connecting to the First Source and Center of all life makes us powerful, hopeful and compassionate. We are all guided by the same Source, no matter what our background.

New Attitude

It is not necessary to change our worldviews in order for us to be a spiritual family together. What has to change is our attitude. Once you improve your attitude, your worldview will soften and you will have more leniency towards people. Families have a level of tolerance towards family members that can bypass a great deal of social strife. Love covers over a multitude of hurts, and if we act like a family and if we work and serve like a family, it will make us stronger because family bonds are the strongest.

Even from a purely biological point of view, we all come from the same primordial soup. All of nature is interconnected through thousands of years of evolutionary history.

It is not necessary for our Freedom Movement to bring our political views to the surface at this time. We can get back to the regular conservative/liberal debate after we win back our freedom. Until then, we need to put much of it aside. For the conservatives in the movement: we cannot win a war on two fronts—we cannot fight both the left and the NWO at the same time. Patriots and progressives in our movement need to both come together, bonded together with the holy glue of love, inspired by the Spirit.

Spirituality vs Religion

We could define spirituality as *religion without borders,* or possibly *religion without institutions.* Much of ancient and mediaeval religion is based on thou-shalt-nots, limits placed on human behavior; these limits are generally beneficial to society such as thou shalt not steal, murder, commit adultery or lie.

The underlying consequence of religious institutions making these limits is that those who break them are considered to have transgressed the institution, its members and society. The ancients taught that this breaks fellowship with God and therefore we need divine intervention, sacrificial killing of animals or some kind of payment to win back the affection of the offended deity.

Spirituality, on the other hand, teaches that we are always one with the universe, we are always a child of God and nature, no matter what our behavior. Neither the universe nor God ever breaks fellowship with us, though we can discontinue our relationship at any time because there is no coercion, compulsion or force used by the divine. We are free to engage with the Source at any time.

Spirituality is generally based on positive commands rather than negative ones. Siddhartha Gautama, for example, taught the 8-fold path of right actions, such as *right speech*, instead of teaching a negative edict to *not swear*. Righteousness or right-doing is not based on refraining from wrong-doing. It is based on doing the right thing.

Our Freedom Movement is composed of *do-gooders* who advocate that our national leaders do the right thing. It is true, however, that we are opposed to the negative commands of our institutional government and health officers who have instructed us with medical thou-shalt-nots, such as thou-shalt-not hug, dance, come within 6 feet of each other or go out without a mask.

Our positive-based approach to health leads us to take vitamins, supplements and exercise regularly to build up our immune system. Our *thou-shalls* are a better plan to overcome a nasty virus, and our movement is fully conscious we are on the right side of history, and that makes us righteous.

Spirituality or *true religion* breaks down boundaries and places fewer limits on people or their behavior. It opens up possibilities and creates relationships instead of dividing people into categories of vaxxed and nonvaxxed, left and right, male and female, gay and straight, Christian and Jew, Muslim and Hindu, New Age and Old Age.

Similar to the Buddha's teachings, Jesus of Nazareth taught positive actions such as, d*o unto others as you would have them do unto you.* He also taught people to love their neighbor in a society where lepers, women, slaves, Gentiles and many others were outcasts.

Spirituality is progressive. It teaches us to grow and serve our friends, family and planet in order to help make our world a better place. Institutional religion is limiting because it first puts people in the physical box of the four walls of a building; and then it puts people in a dogma box that all members are compelled to abide by.

Progress is the watchword of the universe. The entire universe is in perpetual motion, from the smallest atom to the largest solar systems of planets that revolve around mother suns. The universe is designed to be a machine for living that encourages all life to struggle and create new possibilities and new ways of doing things. As the prophet Isaiah said, *"Behold, I will do a new thing. Do you not see it? Now, it shall spring forth. I will make a way in the wilderness and rivers in the desert."*

The Urge to Serve

True spirituality encourages and fosters spiritual growth because as a person matures and grows, he or she becomes more and more useful to the universe and to his or her universe brothers and sisters. The urge to serve is the sign of a growing, motivated believer. The most powerful individual on Earth is a sincere, dynamic, motived spiritualist.

When we become aware we are part of the human family in its quest for higher love and greater purpose, it creates in us a natural desire to serve the family members. This is true of all biological families; the parents naturally want to protect and provide for the children. A family is the basic *peace club*. When we expand our consciousness to include awareness of the whole global human family, then we also expand our level of service to include the whole planet.

Having a universal view of life breaks down barriers and opens us up to new possibilities. Most people have a local worldview and a national worldview. Fewer people have an international worldview, mostly because it's too complicated and takes too much study to understand the complexities of global politics and economics. Very few have the universe view of our place as a planet spinning around a mother sun in an orderly universe.

The urge to serve is always conditioned and informed by the scope and breadth of your worldview. Knowledge and wisdom expands your worldview from the local, to the state/provincial, to the national, international, and finally universal.

In an ideal world, people graduate up the ladder from local to international based on their performance and success at the lower levels. Hereditary corporate monarchs pass on their wealth and power to their children, preventing the rise of average citizens of talent and ability.

The Meaning of Life

All life has a purpose and the main purpose is *to survive*. Every plant, animal and insect on Earth has an innate instinct for self-preservation and to survive as a species by reproduction.

All animal life seeks food, water and shelter because these are the primary requirements for survival. All human life seeks eternal survival at the urging of the activated inner voice. The spirit always wants to return to its home in eternity and we have an innate desire to seek the "kingdom of heaven" led by our soul pilot who knows the way home.

Salvation is survival. There is no guarantee that any sentient freewill creature will move on to the next life for the simple reason that some creatures do not want to go and resist every effort by the spirit who attempts to lead them paradise-ward.

The pathway forward always involves spiritual growth. Maturity means more service to others. An immature nation like an immature person is self-centered instead of service-centered. The carpenter from Nazareth taught in parables with examples from nature: wheat, harvest, seeds, sowing, reaping. All these things involve growing, living things. If someone or something is not growing, it means it is are dying. That's the rule of nature: *all healthy things grow.*

The Role of Revelation

Religion is both evolutionary and revelatory. From the early days of human beings living in caves, there has always been a gradual increase of truth and revelation mixed in with primitive superstition, paganism, animism and fetishism. Everything healthy grows and religion is no exception.

All true spiritual insight is planted in the soil of culture and is therefore destined to become attached to pre-existing world religions. Anyone who is part of an institutional religion can receive genuine knowledge and wisdom from above for *God is no respecter of persons.*

Spiritual revelation or revealed truth is placed in the willing and available mind of any individual who is both receptive and ready to receive it, like a seed planted in the ground. Times of great tribulation, cultural upheaval and transition, like we are experiencing right now, are also times of great revelation. Expect the unexpected because the tyranny that is forcing the world to its knees is also forcing us to push inward to draw upon the well of inspiration and guidance of the great Source and Center.

The Elites want to break the world's spirit and force us into submission to their sociopathic dystopian vision, but we are retreating inward to find guidance and direction. Onwards and *inwards.* There is no countermeasure or defense against the sincere truth-seeker finding solace and communion with the still small voice within.

Our well of inspiration is far more powerful than all the combined media propaganda, manipulation and control that the Elites launch at the world. Good always triumphs over evil. The WEF and their Great Reset are misguided and distorted visions of the future that will never be fulfilled. The only hope for these erring deviants is that they become disillusioned by their quest for power and control, and come over to our side.

EPILOGUE/Empowered Communities

Our world is at the point of no return. If we do not make drastic, fundamental changes to our societies we are doomed to extinction. This is not just alarmist rhetoric, it is the reality of our situation. The Elites who rule our world have gone mad and their insane plans are a slow-motion train wreck leading to complete disaster.

There have been several times in modern history where a course correct was required. Two examples: Despite the lengthy battles to combat resistance, legalized slavery is over and women have the vote throughout the world. These two social justice struggles were fought simultaneously in the late 1800's and the early part of the last century. Many of those who fought for women's rights, such as Susan B. Anthony, also fought for equality for black people.

Our struggle is far more titanic because it is a global tyranny that threatens not only the lives of billions, but also the very soul of humanity. We must resist with all our strength.

And while we are fighting, we also need to start over and have fresh ideas and a new direction. Small empowered communities are one such way to start fresh, and these communities are springing up all over the world, under the radar of the mainstream media and the peering eyes of the global surveillance state.

We discussed freedom cells in the first book in this series, *How to Defeat the New World Order*. Many such small autonomous cell groups have already been established here in Vancouver and throughout the area. This author takes pride in being one of the people facilitating that effort. The larger empowered communities have a different angle and perspective that creates change and opportunity for individuals to become leaders and influencers.

The Union of the People

The Union of the People is one such empowered community in the Vancouver area that has grown over the last few months. The last meeting had over 75 people in attendance, in age from the very young to grandparents. According to the lead organizer, Saadiq Daya, "Union of the People is a diverse array of people working towards a community built on individual empowerment and social synergy."

www.unionofthepeople.com

With a strong emphasis on physical fitness, Union of the People hosts weekly boxing and fitness sessions for youth and adults. Their focus is currently on physical, social and financial health for everyone, rebuilding the foundation that society needs to be built on. "We can't be cogs in a machine, we were meant to all be empowered individuals making up a collective society," Saadiq says their philosophy is based on networking, synergy and community.

He has accepted the fact the ship is sinking and society needs replacing with new ideas. "Rising tides raise all ships. Synergy is needed to start a new community. Humans' strength is synergy. If we put 10 humans in a jungle we're going to take over the jungle. That's what separates us from animals. The core element required is synergy," he continues, "There's a place for everyone. Very important we get together in person. We do not have a lot of delegation and assigning tasks. We break off into committees and brainstorm ideas, thoughts, and problems coming up in the next months and try to break down everything into active or non-active phases. Ideas going into phase one and phase two. The community can solve the problems."

Union of the People meeting. Saadiq Daya addressing the group.

Let's talk about *synergy*, the core of the Union's philosophy. The term synergy comes from the Attic Greek word συνεργία synergia from *synergos*, συνεργός, meaning "co-worker" or "working together." Synergy is an interaction or cooperation giving rise to a whole that is greater than the simple sum of its parts.

This is the basic idea that the group can create something greater than the individuals working separately. In the context of organizational behavior, following the view that a cohesive group is more than the sum of its parts, synergy is the ability of a group to outperform even its best individual member.

Saadiq claims we need to establish our own society independent of the system. "Establishing itself, running little projects. Working on different routes, keeping each other up, helping each others' businesses. When you put multiple people together you get new things that would never have happened if people did not get together. We bring people and ideas together."

The Union has multiple committees in the areas of events, public relations, legal, membership team, business networking, E-commerce sites, monetizing skills and products, and a regular craft fair has begun.

Risky Shift

In behavioral psychology, those who study group dynamics refer to something called *Risky Shift*. This is the tendency for groups of people to choose a riskier policy than what any one individual would choose. This tendency is surprising as it would seem that groups would choose less risky behavior when collective decisions are made, but the opposite is the case.

This tendency also applies in the reverse case, when individuals in the group are advising caution, the group tendency is to decide for greater caution. Psychologists and sociologists called this *group polarization*.

Facebook is a prime example of how public discussion and debate often leads to greater division instead of greater harmony. When people are engaging in posts, the tendency is for individuals to take polarizing opinions a step further to appear as a leader. Then others adopt this new leading opinion which moves the debate further away from compromise and agreement.

Empowered communities need to be aware of these tendencies because it is often the root of division. Avoid the Risky Shift and the Cautious Shift when the group engages in decision-making so that polarization will be avoided. As we discussed in *Part 2 of How to Defeat the New World Order*, the better strategy is to move closer to the center when others are being divisive and promoting extreme positions of fight-or-flight.

The Future

There has never been a time in history when the future of our planet is so much in the hands of the People like it is now. Throughout all of human history, the movers and shakers have mostly been from the ruling-class with notable exceptions such as Gandhi, Buddha, Jesus of Nazareth, Martin Luther King and Confucius.

We are now in the Age of the People.

We must all become mini-Buddhas and micro-Jesus. The new prophets and leaders must come from the broad base of humanity and not from among the elite billionaire-class. We must overthrow them with all our body, soul and strength.

The great hope for humanity is in the simple yet profound law of life summarized by Jesus of Nazareth and other great teachers, that we treat each other the way we want to be treated, that we do unto others as we would have them do unto us. The Golden Rulers must take charge of our planet. Those that are in power currently live by another rule—the rule of "order" and not the rule of Law. They want to reign by arbitrary "community standards" without appeal or justice; the same arbitrary health orders that we witness unelected health officials randomly spewing forth from their pulpits of fake science.

Our mission is plain. We must create a new world on the ashes of the old. As their Empire of Chaos crumbles and falls, we must build the scaffolding of a new society that does not seek power and wealth and war. We must establish a society based on service to others, the rule of law and the brotherhood of all humankind inspired by the great Source and Center of all creation.

The parent, guardian, mother, father of the universe is a breath away, closer than a lover—we only need to connect to the Source and drink up. Then we can act upon the leading and guidance of this same inner voice, this same universal mind, Higher Power and Great Spirit.

This has always been the Way from the dawn of time to the end of eternity. The sun comes up every day and shines upon us. The Earth revolves around the sun and we swing in a grand and majestic arc through the universe of space and time. When we pass from this world to the next, we will awaken on another better world. Until, we must roll up our sleeves and work towards a vision of life and liberty that will take us Beyond the New World Order.

Manufactured by Amazon.ca
Bolton, ON

25476087R00059